EXPLORING WASHINGTON ARCHAEOLOGY

Wall screen from Ozette carved with Wolf and Thunderbird.

Exploring Washington Archaeology

Ruth Kirk with Richard D. Daugherty

Published in cooperation with the Washington State
Office of Archaeology and Historic Preservation

UNIVERSITY OF WASHINGTON PRESS
Seattle and London

To Charles E. Borden and Luther S. Cressman, whose archaeological research has been fundamental to our understanding of
prehistory in the Pacific Northwest.

Library of Congress Cataloging in Publication Data

Kirk, Ruth.
    Exploring Washington archaeology.

    Includes index.
        1. Indians of North America—Washington (State)—
Antiquities. 2. Man, Prehistoric—Washington (State) 3. Wash-
ington (State)—Antiquities. I. Daugherty, Richard D., 1922-
        joint author. II. Title.
E78.W3K48   979.7   78-54012
ISBN 0-295-95630-5
ISBN 0-295-95610-0 pbk.

Preface

Archaeology isn't a treasure hunt—except in the sense that knowledge is treasure beyond equivalence in precious metals or jewels.

The wondrous paintings on cave walls in Spain and France, the riches of Troy, and the funerary trophies of ancient China and Egypt are a part of archaeology; but not the whole. The term derives from the Greek and means "the science of antiquity." Applied to the artwork of the past it means looking not just at images and objects, but probing beyond them to the peoples who produced them, who tried to give form to the insights life held for them. The search for our earliest ancestors at Olduvai Gorge; the study of Pompeii, its life suddenly stopped—and preserved—by volcanic ashfall; Viking ships raised from watery depths; pyramids in Mexico and Central America; cliff-dweller ruins in the United States Southwest; and pithouses and whaling villages in the Northwest—this all falls within the embrace of archaeology.

History bases its tale of our human past on documents. Yet through most of time there have been no documents; most cultures and most of the world's peoples have had no writing. They belong to "prehistory," the time before written documents. This dividing line varies from place to place but nowhere reaches into the past further than five thousand years, the time of writing's origin. In Washington the earliest written records go back to barely over two hundred years ago, a scanty record for a people whose ancestry now is known to reach at least twelve thousand years into the past. Furthermore, the written record here is one seen with alien eyes and set down with at best limited insight, at worst deliberate bias. Archaeological evidence, on the other hand, spans from Washington's early wanderers to its settled villagers. It presents a look at the past of Indian peoples that goes beyond oral tradition, and it deepens the awareness of us all of membership within the family of man. We are a species curious about origins. Archaeology concerns itself with the diversity of our beginnings.

The pages here are no more than a sampling of Washington's past, with an emphasis on archaeological undertakings by Washington State University, owing to the book's authorship. To all who have helped—more numerous than space permits listing—go our thanks. To those whose studies have been drawn upon go acknowledgments of indebtedness.

Ruth Kirk
Richard D. Daugherty
*Washington Archaeological
Research Center*
Pullman, Washington

Wedding Rock petroglyph (above). Wooden comb from Ozette (opposite).

Floodplain excavation at Marmes Rockshelter.

Contents

Bighorn sheep petroglyph, eastern Washington.

The Land

No single description can capture the essence of the landscape of Washington, home of man for a proven twelve thousand years and probably far longer. Take color, for instance. Soft grays and browns characterize the inland sagebrush flats and basalt coulees; greens and blues, the coastal forests and waters. Between the two realms rise the Cascade Mountains. Threading them are the Columbia and Snake rivers, the Skagit and Nooksack and Chehalis and a host of others.

Yet this doesn't begin to describe the succession of stages, upon which the human drama of the state has been set. To visualize one of these stages—one that probably occurred at 13,000 B.P. (which means Before Present)—think of icebergs such as those off today's Alaskan coast afloat on floodwaters seven hundred feet deep near Pasco. For another, say 14,000 B.P., bury Seattle beneath three thousand feet of glacial ice; let that melt, and replace it with a lake reaching to Olympia and draining through the Chehalis Valley to the Pacific. Perhaps 13,000 B.P. and again around 6,700 B.P. whiten eastern Washington not with snow, but with powdery volcanic ash erupted from Glacier Peak and Mount Mazama, Oregon.

Whatever stage man chances to be born onto affects what he needs in order to live well. Must he cope with cold and constant drizzle and snow showers; or is the climate warm, the land dry? Does he show bravery by paddling to sea to hunt whales; or by stampeding bison, or stalking elephants? Do women dig sword fern roots, or biscuit root and bitterroot? Modern archaeology concerns itself with such matters. Man doesn't live in a vacuum, nor is he a singular species. Ours is one life form among many, and our time, even as a species, is but one element in a continuum so vast it staggers the mind. To know ourselves we must know the stages and the cast of the long drama that have led to the present.

The earth is 5 billion years old, and the earliest manlike creatures developed perhaps 2 or 3 million years ago. Population of the western hemisphere began 30,000 to 40,000 years ago. Archaeology is the science of looking at that human time from two perspectives: cultural and environmental.

Consider, for example, the Washington landscape. Immense basalt flows layered one over the other make up the Columbia Plateau, virtually the whole of eastern Washington except for the Okanogan Highlands in the Northeast corner. The flows have directly affected human life. Hollowed at the base of many are caves: natural shelters and storage rooms and burial vaults. In some cases these caves have formed where ancient waterfalls formed plunge pools at the bases of cliffs, undermining the layers. In other cases frost has swollen within cracks and has loosened blocks, opening niches.

Topography and environment—in Washington, richly varied—greatly affect human adaptation. Opposite from top: *Palouse Canyon with Marmes Rockshelter at lower left; Cascade Mountains looking from South Picketts toward Mount Baker; Point of Arches on the outer coast of the Olympic Peninsula with Ozette Island and the Bodeltahs on the horizon. Above: Bone figure from Ozette (shown here about three times actual size).*

The caves close to canyon bottoms served man especially well. Many are fairly easy to scramble up into. Often rivers or ponds are closeby—convenient sources of water and desirable locations for hunting and fishing. Frequently, canyon bends cut off prevailing winds. Southern exposures maximized winter sunshine, eastern exposures assured the earliest possible morning warmth. Things left behind by man, whether from a hunter's overnight camp or a family's seasonal occupancy, usually will be better preserved within a cave than out in the open. Archaeologists can hope to find debris and implements associated with butchering and cooking, bone and stone tools and weapons, pigments, and occasional mats and baskets, although these usually disintegrate within a few centuries.

Molten basalt flowed across the land repeatedly during the Miocene epoch, from 25 to 13 million B.P. It welled up not from volcanic peaks, but from fissures up to several miles long. It was a fairly fluid lava and filled low places, crusting over with flat, even tops. The combined flows buried the earlier surfaces so deeply that geologists have little idea of eastern Washington's previous topography. Individual layers are as much as two hundred feet thick. The quantity of molten rock involved in them is staggering. A single flow spred across twenty thousand square miles; it extends from near Grand Coulee east to Spokane, south to Pendleton, Oregon, and southwest to the Columbia River Gorge.

Cooling was slow. Probably the rock solidified inward at a rate of only about ten feet per year. Particularly toward the bottom of some flows this produced conspicuous shrinkage cracks, giving these cliff faces the look of giant rock columns standing tight against one another. Gas bubbles trapped in the cooling rock remain as fossil hollows ranging from pinhole size to a foot or more in diameter. Over the millennia silica has collected in many of these, opalized, and become the raw material of man's spearpoints and arrowheads, knives and scrapers. The basalt itself has been used by man from earliest times for tools and weapons, bowls and pestles and effigies. Obsidian, the volcanic glass widely prized for points and blades is not to be found in Washington. It has a different mineral structure than basalt and because of its vitreous nature it tends to flake to an extraordinarily sharp edge. Obsidian artifacts are found in the state, but only as imports, indicating trade. They therefore hold a fascination and significance distinct from those objects made of locally obtainable materials. Oregon and British Columbia are the sources of obsidian nearest to Washington.

In many parts of the Plateau, deposits of loess blanket the basalt flows. This is wind-blown sediment that rode prevailing northwesterlies from the White Bluffs area near Hanford and the Pasco Basin to settle into low, voluptuously contoured hills. Drive through the Washington wheat fields in spring and the loess lies so rich a brown that even nonfarmers appreciate its obvious fertility. In excavation walls the sediments can be identified as wind-deposited by grain size and other characteristics. Where surfaces have remained stable long enough for soil to develop and plants to grow, that record too will be present even in cross section. Similarly, old river courses and lake beds are discernible. Waterlaid silts settle from slack water, sands and gravels from running water. The coarser the material, the greater the velocity of the water.

Geologists read such clues and consequently are increasingly an integral part of archaeological teams. If, for instance, deposits being investigated hold ancient lake shores lying deep within them, these could be promising places to look for signs of man. Conversely, there is little likelihood of tracing extensive human presence on the surface of former sand dunes. Shifting sand probably long since will have destroyed much of the evidence. Man generally preferred to live where water, fuel, and food resources were readily available—a combination widely obtainable in Washington.

As part of the permanent documentation of archaeological deposits actual columns can be pulled from excavation walls with all layers intact. These permit convenient reference to the precise sequence and nature of deposits even long after field work is completed. The technique is simple. Let resin soak into a vertical section of wall, usually a place where strata are particularly clear and have special significance. When the resin has hardened, cut the sides of the column free, let more resin soak in, and place a board against the face of the section. Gingerly cut the column free from the wall and tie it to the board. Wrap with burlap or plastic sheeting and take the whole to the laboratory for additional resin treatment and study. Such columns form a permanent "library" of stratigraphy.

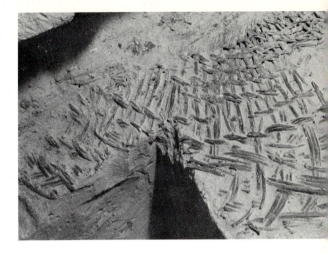

Basalt flows layered one on top of another characterize the Columbia Plateau (opposite, above), many of them with small caves at their bases (opposite, below; this page, below). Archaeologists found a basket while excavating in one such cave near the Snake River—a rare discovery since fiber usually decays quickly (this page, above). The cave had been occupied intermittently for more than 6,700 years: artifacts lay beneath Mazama ash.

Soil columns stabilized with vinylite resin and taken from excavation walls form part of the archaeological record. Actual samples of strata, they afford verification of written records and an opportunity for additional study even after excavation is complete.

Volcanic ash often is present in Washington archaeological deposits. Mount St. Helens, youngest of the Cascades volcanoes, has spewed out ash more than fifty times during the last sixty thousand years. Glacier Peak and Mount Mazama ashes also are frequent and widespread; those from Mount Baker, Mount Rainier, and Newberry Crater, Oregon are fairly restricted and of limited use archaeologically. Each ashfall has its own character, at least theoretically distinguishable by chemical, petrographic, and light refractive means. In practice, identification can be extremely difficult, although techniques recently have been aided by developments in electron probe microscopy.

Since volcanic ash serves as a dependable time marker, these developments have been a real boon for archaeology. Whatever strata lie beneath undisturbed ash obviously are older than the ash itself, and whatever lies above it will be younger. This provides a relative chronology. Dating in terms of years comes from radiocarbon analysis of wood charred on contact with hot ash, and from peat bogs associated with fresh ashfalls. The more ashes that can be identified and precisely dated, the more sound is the archaeological chronology.

Even indications of past climate can be traced within the earth. Examples are polygonal patterns caused by freezing which were found in the floor of excavation squares at the Marmes site in southeastern Washington. They had formed ten thousand years ago when continental ice still lingered along the Canadian border. Washington State University archaeologists pulled soil peels with the polygons, following much the same method as that for soil columns. They soaked the floor of a square with latex rubber, then covered it with thin cloth. More latex went on to bond the cloth to the earth. When it dried, a veneer of undisturbed sediment was peeled free with the cloth as backing.

Just why climate chills enough to produce ice ages isn't fully understood, although it is clear that within the last two million years glaciers repeatedly have mantled much of the planet. Even today nearly 10 percent of the earth's land surface lies beneath ice—an area equivalent to that now being farmed. The basic cause of ice ages most likely relates to aspects of our orbit around the sun. Coinciding cycles reduce incoming warmth and cause snow periodically to whiten the high elevations and high latitudes. With sufficient depth the snow compacts to ice and begins to spread out, driven by the pressure of its own mass. The best evidence is that Earth now is poised at the threshold of a long period of increasing cold. What we don't know is whether incidental results of our technology, such as pollution, will speed chilling or induce warming.

Each ice-age glaciation largely wipes the slate clean of evidence left by its predecessors. Oncoming ice overrides deposits left by previous ice. It sculpts rock, bulldozes loose sediment, and reshapes landforms. Its meltwater reworks and redeposits silts and sands and gravels. What is best understood about glaciation is whatever happened most recently. In Washington this means the events of about 16,000 to 13,000 b.p., and even those events, particularly details such as when melting took place, are just beginning to be understood. The importance of this information to archaeology is obvious. Early man couldn't live under the ice. He could, however, live surprisingly close to its edge. Glacier margins aren't necessarily sterile, as witness the juxtaposition of ice and life in, for example, Glacier Bay, Alaska.

Frost cracks found deep within floodplain deposits at the Marmes site formed 10,000 years ago when worldwide climate was colder than now. At an even lower level geologists encountered a gravel bar left in the wake of an outburst flood that swept across eastern Washington when an ice dam collapsed, releasing 500 cubic miles of water.

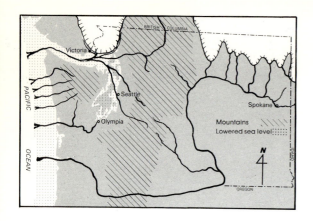

Washington about 20 to 18,000 B.P. Ice that had accumulated in the mountains of western Canada—called Cordilleran ice—was advancing into northwestern United States. It repeatedly dammed the Clark Fork River and broke loose, releasing stupendous floods that swept southwestward from the Spokane region. Glaciers in the Cascade and Olympic mountains were at their maximum. They had advanced down river valleys to the fronts of the mountains, and some extended onto the lowlands as great tongues. Sea level stood perhaps 300 or 400 feet lower than currently, and broad flat plains stretched seaward from today's saltwater shores.

The ice sheet capping western Canada bulged into Washington sometime about 16,000 B.P., the most recent of several similar occurrences. This ice extended across the crest of the Cascade Range, connecting immense western ice lobes in the Strait of Juan de Fuca and the Puget lowlands with a lobe on the Okanogan highlands, which reached in an arc from Lake Chelan to Grand Coulee, and to another lobe east of Spokane. The effects of the glacier extended beyond the ice itself. For instance, the winds that carried the loess onto the Plateau were generated, in part, by warm air suddenly chilled against the miles-long glacial front. The famed Dry Falls of Grand Coulee, and indeed much of the coulee itself, also formed as an indirect result of the glaciation. The Okanogan lobe acted as a gigantic dam and diverted the Columbia River considerably south of its normal course. Its flow, together with melt from the glacier, drained southward through Moses Coulee. Some water also coursed down Grand Coulee, and it long has been supposed that this flow carved the coulee. Recent evidence, however, indicates that most of the coulee's formation came from torrential floods which swept across the state from east of Spokane. The ice lobe there several times dammed the Clark Fork River along the Idaho/Montana border. Lakes impounded by this dam tended to break out abruptly, one time discharging five hundred cubic miles of water. Channels and potholes and ripples from this outburst are still evident from the air, their mark clear, as though formed by bulldozers. The greatest sculpturing of Grand Coulee seems to have been the result of the flood waters, which ultimately produced a cataract four miles wide. The lip and plunge pool of this falls still remain—a Niagara gone dry.

Icebergs rode the flood torrents from the east carrying rocks frozen fast into them. Boulders thus rafted (termed glacial erratics) were carried to near Pasco, about two hundred miles from the Clark Fork. At Lind Coulee northeast of Warden, men who arrived four millennia after the flood used its erratic granite cobbles to pound red ochre for use as some sort of paint. Seemingly there have been at least five such catastrophic floods from 50,000 to 13,000 years ago, the dates indicated by various volcanic ashes. Other floods quite clearly flowed more gently across the land without drastically eroding it.

Glacial erratic boulders in northcentral Washington.

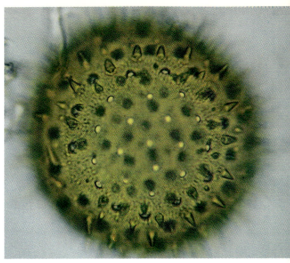

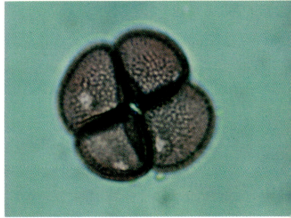

Identification of microscopic particles such as volcanic ash and plant pollen yields dating and environmental information. Mount St. Helens (left) has produced twelve distinct types of ashfall from perhaps sixty separate eruptions. A layer of Mazama ash (below) from the eruption that formed Crater Lake, Oregon provides a time marker of 6,700 years before the present. Archaeological deposits beneath the ash already were in place when the eruption occurred; those above it formed afterward. Pollen grains (above) recovered layer by layer from within the ground tell of vegetation through time: (clockwise) fossil spruce, pine, and fir; mallow; cattail.

The Columbia Plateau of eastern Washington offered human hunters and foragers a protein base that included fish, river mussels, waterfowl (top right), deer and other mammals (lower right). A rich variety of starchy roots available for the digging included camas (middle right) and bitterroot (middle left and below). Columnar basalt and sagebrush are typical of the Plateau (opposite page).

Earliest evidence of man in eastern Washington is from about 10,000 years ago at Marmes Rockshelter (right). Tools and faunal remains 9,000 years old, including part of a bison skull and eggshells, have come from Lind Coulee (this page).

The bones of a mastodon hunted by man nearly 12,000 years ago were discovered on the Olympic Peninsula near Sequim. A tooth (bottom left) establishes positive identification as mastodon, not mammoth. Bone fragments (top) were recovered from the initial excavation. They include part of a rib with a bone spearpoint broken off in it (bottom right).

Early Man in Washington

What Clare and Emanuel Manis wanted was a resting pond for wild ducks and geese. What they got was a mastodon skeleton and one of the major archaeological digs of the Northwest and perhaps the new world.

The couple, who had just moved to the northern Olympic Peninsula near Sequim, built a house on high ground with views to the mountains and the Strait of Juan de Fuca. That was 1975. Two years later, having noticed the wintertime flooding of a low place in the front yard, the Manises decided to turn the quagmire into a pond. With a backhoe Manis stripped off mucky peat from the upper three or four feet of his pond-to-be, and piled it outside the growing perimeter. To drain seepage he dug below the peat layer, scooping out brown earth and gray glacial silt and gravel, which he piled within the perimeter.

In the process he lifted out chunks of bone and what seemed to be a tree trunk or limb. Then out came a second limblike piece. Each was about six inches in diameter and one was four feet long, the other six and one-half feet long. Each was white on the broken tip—obviously tusks from a mammoth or mastodon. Such discoveries have been remarkably frequent on the northern Olympic Peninsula through the years but, recent arrivals, the Manises had no reason to see their chance discovery in relation to these others. Nonetheless, they realized its potential value beyond mere curiosity, and Clare Manis started phoning in search of appropriate experts.

The local high school biology teacher told her to keep the tusks wet or they'd crumble to dust. A librarian suggested contracting Dr. Richard Daugherty, Washington State University professor and director of the Makah-Ozette archaeology project on the west coast of the Olympic Peninsula. Word got to him as he was leaving that site to head back to Pullman, and he detoured to the Manis property as he drove through Sequim. Word also reached Dr. Carl Gustafson, zoologist with the Department of Anthropology at WSU, and with Delbert Gilbow, a graduate student, he too headed for Sequim.

It was mid–August 1977. Everybody expected a three- or-four-day recovery of a few random bones. Gustafson and Gilbow loaded their truck with the gear they expected to need. Not until five months later did they reload it and return to the university campus. The quick recovery had become a major excavation likely to continue for years.

The first sign that the project would be lengthy came only hours after work got underway. Gustafson, Gilbow, and Daugherty were hosing the mud from which the two tusks had come, their immediate task the salvage of additional chunks of tusk and bone broken by the backhoe. Dr. Gustafson washed free a seven-inch piece of rib and picked it up to examine. Almost instinctively he knew he had something beyond the ordinary. A broken piece of bone nearly the size of a man's fingertip projected from the rib, seemingly the remnant of a spearpoint. To become imbedded into the rib it had to have cut through several inches of tough hide and muscle.

Gustafson borrowed a microscope from the Sequim high school, and he and Daugherty examined their prize. The intrusive bone showed as more dense than the rib bone and lacking periostium, the outer covering that is easily worn off in the process of tool manufacture. Tiny flakes of rib appeared bent over and tucked into the wound by impact. The wound's edges showed signs of healing. Later X-ray examination, volunteered by the Wallace Harms Laboratory in Bellevue, demonstrated this clearly. Three or four months would be needed in human bone to reach that stage; in bone from an extinct animal, who can say?

The healing proved both that the spear thrust hadn't been fatal and that the wound wasn't a post-mortem occurrence. Furthermore, the dark X-ray shadow of the instrusive fragment showed it to be pointed and jammed nearly an inch into the rib. There seemed to be no possibility of its having gotten there by any means other than man's intentional act.

Aerial photograph of the Manis property shows the outline of the aborted duckpond. Twelve thousand years ago the Sequim area was dotted by kettle lakes that formed as stagnant ice slowly melted. One such lake, long since filled with sediments and peat, contained the mastodon skeleton.

Seemingly the mastodon was an aged one for many of the bones showed the rough knobs and "lipping" of arthritis. However it died, man evidently had used it for food. Several bones showed signs of butchering, and by the time excavation stopped for the winter the skull had been located. It lay smashed into hundreds of pieces. Probably humans had removed the brain to eat or, if they followed the practices of their likely descendants in recent times, to use it in tanning hides. The orientation of the skull was 180° from the live position of the head, twisted to face backwards, and upside down as well. In addition, ribs underlay the left tibia, the forty- or fifty-pound bone of the lower hind leg. This position, too, would have been impossible while alive or as the result of any imaginable geologic process.

Until excavation of the skeleton is complete, details of how the animal died can't be known. At archaeological sites such as Blackwater Draw in New Mexico and Lehner in Arizona, evidence indicates that hunters may have hurled rocks at the heads of mired mammoths. In Africa today Pygmies hunt elephants by creeping close and jabbing spears up into the soft underbelly. The technique isn't intended to kill outright but to incapacitate. Hunters then track their wounded prey and deliver the *coup de grace* in due time. Men may or may not have used these techniques in attacking the Manis mastodon.

That the skeleton is mastodon, not mammoth, became clear on the third day of excavation when a molar was found. Mastodons seemingly fed on the leaves of brush and perhaps herbs, but not so much on grass. Their cheek teeth—twelve in all—are thinly covered with enamel and subject to cavities, wear, and loss, as are human teeth. The grit inevitable in a grass diet would have been ruinous for them. It is the teeth, about the size of a human fist, that give the animal its name, originally spelled "mastodont." The word incorporates the Greek *odon*, "tooth," with *mastos*, "breast" (for the cusps on the teeth). The Manis molar was worn to the gumline, further indication of an aged animal, and a cavity pocked the chewing surface.

To prevent their crumbling before proper preservation could be carried out, the mastodon tusks were kept in an impromptu pool of water scooped into the ground and lined with plastic (left). Dr. Carl Gustafson and Dr. Richard Daugherty used a microscope to examine the bone spearpoint found on the third day of excavation (right). It had passed through the mastodon's tough hide and several inches of flesh, imbedding in a rib. This would have required considerable force, suggestion that the spear had been hurled with an atlatl rather than by hand and arm alone.

Mammoth teeth differ substantially from mastodon teeth. They are larger, set one on each side of the upper and lower jaws, and are self-replacing, somewhat as are sharks' teeth. Instead of cusps, they have hard ridges of enamel that extend to the roots. Abrasion from grit poses no real problem, and apparently mammoths fed extensively on grass.

Wet conditions have preserved the bones, tusks, and teeth of the Manis mastodon. Ancient pollen grains and seeds also remain, some of the seeds large enough to collect, although doing so proved tedious. Nearly two cupfuls were needed for radiocarbon dating, an immense quantity picked one pinhead-size seed at a time from cold, wet mud.

The dating method, commonly known as carbon-14, measures the time of organic death. It is effective to 35,000 B.P. or to twice that age through a recently developed process of thermal separation. It works best with plant material, including charcoal, less well with bone and shell. The particular seeds at the Manis site warranted gathering because they belonged to a pondweed. This is important. The quantity of seeds present in the deposits could only have come from plants growing right there. They weren't blown in from somewhere else, neither were they washed in by chance, for hairlike appendages still were attached. The seeds' date would faithfully represent the age of the deposits in which the mastodon lay.

Initial carbon-14 dates of slightly over twelve thousand years came from the seeds and some wood found with them. This fit with what Dr. Gustafson and Dr. Daugherty expected when they first looked at the strata cut by the backhoe. At that time they could see undisturbed glacial deposits, then the bones lying in reworked glacial deposits, and on top of that a layer of muck. Seemingly the mastodon had died in a small pond perhaps formed by meltwater from a block of stagnant ice.

Pollen contemporaneous with the mastodon is dominantly cattail and sedge. WSU palynologists Dr. Peter Mehringer and Kenneth Petersen came to the site to collect samples. Pollen is so minute and widespread that a bit of earth no bigger than a human fingernail will have enough in it for identification. In order to work out the full spectrum of vegetation through time, the two men took a vertical column of the trench wall from top to bottom and from this at half-inch intervals they prepared microscope slides. In addition to cattail and sedge, they found grass, pondweed, some wild rose and blackberry, Canadian buffalo-berry (a bush typical of the subarctic northland today), willow (probably a shrub species), and alder (quite possibly the Sitka alder common on recently deglaciated land along the present Alaska coast—a low, tough, sinuous growth even more detested by hikers than the salal of the Washington and British Columbia coasts).

Mammoths (above) are more directly related to present-day elephants than are mastodons (below). Plant remains associated with mastodon bones in the Great Lakes region and along the Atlantic coast almost always include conifers, especially spruce. At Sequim, however, overall vegetation at the time of the mastodon was tundralike and without trees. Cattail pollen was present in pond deposits, and lengths of cattail stems may actually represent stomach contents, indication of what the mastodon ate the day it died.

The climate at the time the mastodon died must have been like that where such plants grow now: cool, with brief moderate summers. Anyone familiar with today's far north would recognize the environment. Even the scene of 12,000 years ago was much like that of the present subarctic. East of Sequim the ice from Canada was thicker and therefore slower to melt than in lower Puget Sound. Remnants still lingered on the northeastern peninsula, and part of the land between there and Sequim had not yet been free of ice long enough to get beyond the pioneer stage of reconquest by plants. To the south, the glaciers of the Olympic Mountains already had retreated well up their valleys in response to the general warming. Local conditions within some drainages may have triggered re-advances but not enough so for ice to have approached Sequim; no alpine glacier deposits are found overlying those of the continental ice sheet.

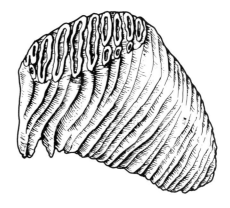

Sea level was lower than what it now is. A broad plain stretched northward far beyond today's shore. Sequim Bay didn't exist, and Protection Island stood as an abrupt hill conspicuously isolated; the Strait of Juan de Fuca was narrowed. The ice sheet by then had withdrawn to about the Gulf Islands/Blaine vicinity, and bergs calved from it quite certainly rode the currents and washed ashore on the Washington coast.

Today's Chamber of Commerce might have to rewrite their advertising for Sequim, but the mastodon hunters had no reason to feel theirs was a hard life in an inhospitable realm. Within mere decades after the disappearance of ice the chain of life rebuilds. By 12,000 B.P. a variety of big animals were grazing and browsing the northern Olympic Peninsula. In addition to the mastodon bones, a caribou antler came from the Manis excavations. So did the molar of an immature bison and bones with green-stick fractures, probably from the same animal. This type of break is a common result of man's butchering, extracting marrow, or getting a piece of bone to work into a tool.

In addition to the spearpoint still imbedded in the rib, WSU archaeologists found one other piece of bone cut to a blunt point, apparently by man, and several flat pieces of tusk smoothly beveled and polished along the edges in a way that couldn't have happened while the mastodon was alive or by accident after its death.

All excavation was done with spray from hoses, using water pumped from seepage into the would-be pond. This method freed the fragile bones without harm; hard tools such as shovels or trowels would have damaged them no matter how carefully used, and archaeologists' brushes, so useful in dry deposits, are worthless in mud. As bones and tusk fragments were washed free and taken to the field laboratory, they were cleaned and soaked in a preservative of vinylite resin. At the end of January, when excavation stopped in favor of time for analysis and regrouping, most of the pieces were taken to Pullman for detailed measurement and study. Excavation was scheduled to resume in early June. Two-thirds of the skeleton still awaited recovery, and Daugherty and Gustafson hoped to find additional artifacts and—with luck—a campsite used by the men who hurled the spear.

Teeth reflect diet. The ridges of mammoth teeth (above) provided a shearing surface, whereas the cusps of mastodon teeth (below) were for grinding. In both, the height of the crown is related to the ability to withstand wear—and the Manis molar was worn to the gumline, indication of an aged animal. Teeth are the most frequently discovered evidence of extinct elephants. Complete skeletons are rare except under unique preservation circumstances such as those of the tar pits of southern California and the permafrost of Siberia.

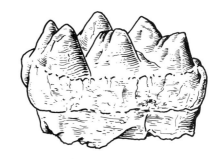

Pumps were used to remove water from the backhoe trench. Before beginning to excavate, archaeologists carefully examined the stratigraphy. Clearly, the mastodon bones rested on glacial till.

Discoveries such as this mastodon and evidence of its hunters have great value in filling gaps in our understanding of the past. Their importance is public, but on private land the decision as to what should happen is up to the individual owner. On state and federal land no construction can be undertaken without first ascertaining that archaeological or historic remains won't be disturbed. All private collecting and excavating without permit is forbidden as a means of protecting the heritage of us all for the enlightenment and enjoyment of us all.

The mastodon find ranks as major. Most of the previous extinct elephant discoveries in Washington—and throughout the nation—have been of mammoths, a close relative of the modern elephants of Africa and India. None of these had been a whole skeleton (except possibly for one near Pomeroy which a road crew considered in the way and summarily shoved into the ditch with a bulldozer). Preservation seldom is good enough for more than a few bones to remain, a factor that made the Manis discovery beneath wet muck particularly promising right at the outset. Continuously wet—or continuously dry—conditions offer the best chances of preservation. Alternation between the two speeds destruction.

Mammoths and mastodons, which are no more than distant cousins of each other, are old-world forms that crossed to America via one of the early land bridges from Siberia to Alaska. Mammoths tend to be the larger. The biggest example known stood fourteen and one-half feet at the shoulder. Late Pleistocene mammoths were smaller than this, typically ten to eleven feet at the shoulder, and the mastodons of that time were smaller still, seldom over seven or eight feet high. Dr. Gustafson's preliminary measurements, however, show the Manis mastodon to be about 10 percent larger than most of its known contemporaries.

Both of these ancient forms of elephant are extinct but are widely known from paleontological specimens including, in the case of mammoths, remarkably intact, frozen carcasses found in northeast Siberia in such numbers that trade in their ivory formerly was a thriving industry. The mammoths were well suited to subarctic conditions by virtue of a thick fat layer under the skin and an outer coat of soft wool plus an overlying thatch of hair. Their ears were smaller than elephants' doubtless to reduce body heat loss; their trunks were short. Mammoths are one of the few extinct animals of which we can know details of the fleshy part of the body, not just the bony parts. The frozen carcasses make this possible. Mastodons can't be as well known.

There were four separate species of mammoth in the New World during the time that man too was present. Only one mastodon species survived in North America into the late Pleistocene and perhaps three in South America (which mammoths never reached). Across the United States and Canada mastodons are found particularly in eastern woodlands and to a lesser extent in northern Florida and Texas where coniferous forest previously flourished. In Washington only occasional scattered bones and one or two tusks had been identified prior to the Sequim excavations.

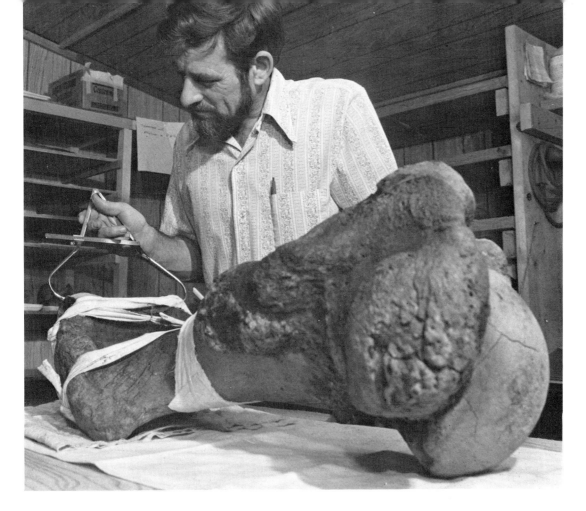

Humerus of the mastodon (above); tibia in situ (below). The Manis mastodon lay on its left side. The right, uppermost side was extensively butchered, its bones piled in a heap. Archaeologists found a stone chopping or cutting tool lying near them.

Mammoth kill sites are not uncommon but, for unknown reasons, no mastodon kill sites had been found in all of the western hemisphere until the late 1970s. Archaeologists supposed that man must have hunted mastodons, but they had no evidence. Now there are two such possible sites newly located in Central and South America as well as the one in North America. In Guatemala a few stone flakes were found associated with mastodon bones, perhaps indication of human hunting. In Venezuela, the summer before the Manis discovery, Dr. Alan Bryan, of the University of Alberta, found the mid-section of a broken projectile point lying in the pubic cavity of a partly dismembered mastodon. A chert flake nearby seemed associated with an ulna (foreleg bone). The deposits, which date to about 13,000 B.P., must have been continuously wet, for "short, sheared twigs evidently chewed by the beast were in association with the rest," Dr. Bryan wrote to Dr. Daugherty.

Mastodons and mammoths lived for millions of years then they were gone not only from America but worldwide. Most of this extinction was complete by 10,000 to 8,000 B.P. although a few mastodons probably survived in scattered pockets until perhaps as late as 6,000 B.P. Dozens of other vertebrates from all continents and major islands also seem to have vanished during the late Pleistocene. Similar die-offs occurred near the ends of the Cretaceous and Pliocene epochs but they appear less extensive, although evidence is limited and obscure. In any case, at the end of the Pleistocene more than thirty entire genera disappeared from North America alone during a five-thousand-year span. This seems abrupt, although Dr. Gustafson points out that we humans count a genus as extinct when we find its last species gone. Far from a sudden occurrence, the process itself may have been underway for a long time. Endings are as normal as beginnings. Individuals die. Populations die. Species and genera and even whole families die. For example, dinosaurs lived 100 million years, yet had been extinct for 60 million years before the first mammoths migrated from Africa to Eurasia.

Pleistocene fauna was more varied overall than is true of current fauna, and it included more large species. Also because of differences in climate and vegetation, distribution was not the same as now. Caribou (top, above), and bison (below) were present at Sequim as the last ice age closed. This is known from remains found at the Manis site, including several bison molars (center).

Apply this principle to the Pleistocene, however, and argument only begins since there is some indication that extinctions were peculiarly concentrated at the end of that epoch. If true, what new factor had become operative? The answer could be man. For millions of years the various elephantlike animals of America, native horses, camels, rhinoceroses, and a host of other mammals had crossed to and from Eurasia during the times that Beringia stood above water. Yet not long after man crossed to the new world, wholesale extinction set in. Overhunting must be the explanation, according to one line of reasoning. America isn't alone in this regard. Mass extinction also took place shortly after man arrived in Europe from Africa; and soon after he got to Australia, New Zealand, and Madagascar.

This is true, but more coincidental than causative counters another line of thought. Man the hunter could have been no more than a factor toppling an already precarious balance. Or it may have been man the destroyer that amounted to the classic "last straw." Both intentionally and accidently he has burned enormous tracts of land in Europe, beginning even before the onset of the last ice age. The preponderance of grasslands in some regions may even derive from man's fires.

Even so, human beings didn't initiate Pleistocene extinction, these investigators say. That came from the environmental flux that accompanied the change in climate. After all, the end of the ice age meant not only the wasting of glaciers in the north but the drying of lakes and the dying of forests in the south. It was this loss of habitat that did the killing along with unaccustomed temperature fluctuations. The Pleistocene climate had been cool, moist, and monotonous. But as it ended conditions began to range from cold to hot on a night-to-day and a seasonal basis. The combination of reduction in suitable habitat and the temperature fluctuation was stressful. Animals too specialized to cope with change died out. Those flexible in behavior survived. The new environment simply had re-set the evolutionary clock. Nothing extraordinary or wholly unprecedented was involved.

One adaptation to dwindling habitat is to develop smaller body size. Largeness per se characterized Pleistocene fauna, perhaps partly in response to the cold since small bodies aren't desirable in arctic conditions. Too great a proportion of internal warmth is lost to the atmosphere. By the end of the ice age, however, dwarfism had proliferated: a small body makes less demand on remaining environmental resources. It may even be that the so-called giant bison and giant elk hunted by early man in eastern Washington and across the plains were direct ancestors of modern bison and elk and not distinct species as they usually are considered. Smaller size may simply reflect environmental adaptation, not a change in species.

By the close of the Pleistocene the hunters who depended for their livelihood on the herds of large grazing animals had become a widespread people already populating South America. Probably little archaeological evidence of them ever will be found because these early people were few in number and lived as scattered bands with limited material possessions.

Elephant discoveries in Washington heretofore have been limited to partial skeletons, such as a tusk salvaged from deposits near the Tri-Cities.

Excavation at Lind Coulee has permitted recovery of a more complete tool inventory than has been true at other Washington sites of comparable age. Also, Lind Coulee is the earliest major site known on the Columbia Plateau away from the Columbia or Snake rivers.

In western Washington the Manis archaeological site is the earliest known so far. In eastern Washington two sites have yielded substantial human evidence radiocarbon dated from at least 9,000 and 10,000 B.P. These are Lind Coulee and Marmes Rockshelter. Glimpses of occupation belonging to about the same time have come from scattered locations such as Little's Landing near Wenatchee, Kettle Falls on the upper Columbia River, and Windust Cave, Granite Point, and Thorn Thicket on the lower Snake River.

All of these eastern Washington sites demonstrate an aspect of archaeologists' search that is less than ideal: imminent destruction largely has dictated where to look. This is because early man, recent man, and current man all have concentrated land use along river valleys—and for the same reasons. Valleys provide water supply, good fishing, level land for living, and a gentle gradient for transport whether afloat or on foot. Drastic change accompanies present-day utilization of river valleys, including reservoirs which flood the cultural remnants left by our predecessors.

In 1946, with the Columbia Basin irrigation project getting underway, the Smithsonian Institution began sponsoring surveys to assess potential damage to paleontological and archaeological deposits. As part of their surveys Richard Daugherty, at the time still a graduate student, went to Lind Coulee with others to look at some bison bones reported in a bank ten to fifteen feet below ground level. Pieces of flaked stone protruded from the coulee wall near the bones.

The following summer, and again in 1950, Daugherty excavated at nearby Moses Lake and from there returned to look again at Lind Coulee, which is near Warden. In the summers of 1951 and 1952 he directed a full-scale excavation. The bison bones and flakes found earlier seemed promising to him partly because of lime coating them with a fairly thick crust that must have taken considerable time to accumulate. Radiocarbon dating confirmed this, giving an age of 8,700 ± 400. (The plus-minus figure indicates the range of accuracy.) Charring of the bone suggested association with man. So did the presence of other bones, still articulated, as though hunters had butchered a kill and carried a few choice portions back to camp. Stone knives and projectile points and scrapers lay in the deposits with the bones.

Under this layer were waterlaid sediments that showed no trace of cultural material. Boulders weighing five hundred pounds or more rested with their bases in this sediment, their tops extending up into the zone with the artifacts and bison bones. The boulders had been ice-rafted by the last of the great floods. Several stone tools stood on edge as if they had been dropped into soft sand and stayed in that position while sediments built around them. Probably the site had served as a camp close beside a stream.

In all, Daugherty and the crew recovered 186 artifacts in the two summers of work. Of these, one set of implements seemed to whisper of the past with particular immediacy: the handstones, or manos, still stained with paint. There were four of these—granite cobbles that would fit comfortably into the hand. Only two pallets were found, each a rectangle of thin basalt. One still had back-and-forth scratchmarks, indication that someone had ground paint 9,000 years ago. Pigment was found too: fourteen pieces of red hematite and one of yellow limonite.

Only four bone tools came from the excavations, one of them a serrated fragment almost three inches long with four teeth angling in one direction and a fifth hooked back the opposite way. The notches were scarred, as though cut by a stone blade. They also were rounded and polished, perhaps by sawing a grit-laden string back and forth against the bone. Dr. Daugherty thought this must have been used somehow for hunting small game such as rabbits or muskrats, or perhaps for spearing fish or birds.

With a small but extremely significant sample recovered from the site, operations stopped, and energy—and funds—were directed elsewhere. Then in the early 1970s Lind Coulee excavations reopened for four field seasons with Ann Irwin, a WSU archaeologist, as project director. The coulee was being used as a wasteway for the Columbia Basin irrigation project and runoff from irrigated fields, plus seepage from livestock ponds, were soaking into the archaeological deposits. If any additional material, particularly bone, ever was to be recovered, the time had come. The moisture would destroy bone artifacts and faunal remains that had been dry for thousands of years. Excavation got underway again. Instead of the dusty site Daugherty had known in the 1950s, Ann Irwin and her crew found slowly flowing water and inviting greenery. The little coulee had reverted to much the same conditions that must have existed 9,000 years ago.

Serrated bone points found at Lind Coulee may have been used to spear small mammals, birds, or fish.

Needles ranked as perhaps the most singular discovery of the renewed work. They are bone, and about the size of modern steel embroidery needles. Skill went into the shaping and sharpening of the bone and the drilling of the tiny holes for the eyes. Twelve needles and needle blanks were found in all, most of them broken. Probably they were intended for making tailored skin clothing. The climate still was cool. The ice cap of earlier millennia had melted from Washington but still lingered in British Columbia. Warm garments must have meant survival, and finding the needles used to make them gave a special satisfaction. With many artifacts archaeologists can only speculate regarding use, but a needle requires no analogue.

Radiocarbon dates from the new excavation matched the approximate 9,000 B.P. date obtained previously. The site still appeared to be a hunter's camp with either the same people, or some extremely close culturally, returning year after year to hunt. Probably it was in spring for the bones of fetal and young bison and elk predominated over those of mature animals. Also, there were broken shells from goose-sized eggs.

Between the two periods of excavation at Lind Coulee, important disoveries had come from Marmes Rockshelter in the southeast corner of the state near Palouse Falls. In age these ranged from recent decades to sometime earlier than 10,000 B.P., the cultural sequence as significant as the antiquity. The setting was the Palouse River near its confluence with the Snake River.

As part of the program of salvage along rivers to be dammed, Dr. Daugherty had excavated a village at the mouth of the Palouse River and tested nearby rock shelters. The Marmes Rockshelter, named for the family who owned the property, seemed promising enough that three summers of work went into it between 1962 and 1964. Then the time came to move on. Daugherty knew of more than eighty sites in need of investigation within the basin of Lower Monumental Reservoir alone. The rock shelter continued to be used as a demonstration site for students, however.

Artifacts and burials reaching back 8,000 years had come from the cave floor, possible to date approximately even without carbon-14 analysis because they lay beneath undisturbed ash from Mount Mazama. That particular eruption, which gave birth to Crater Lake about 6,700 B.P. spewed out debris that carried all the way into Canada and settled to earth as a suffocating blanket of white—a telltale layer useful for dating archaeological deposits.

Working backwards through time the record within the rock shelter floor went from the ranching era, with bits of wire and buttons and shotgun cartridges, to the period of first contact between settlers and Indians. Artifacts included arrowheads beautifully flaked and notched from chert and chalcedony. Deeper within the floor lay projectile points of basalt and also grooved stone weights that had been tied to the shafts of atlatls, or spear throwers. Flat stone mortars lay with pestles, indication that women had learned to gather berries, seeds, and roots and to grind and pound them for food. Scrapers suggested knowledge of how to tan hides for clothing and for waterbags and other containers. Carl Gustafson identified animal bones from the cave floor, finding elk, deer, bighorn sheep, pronghorn, coyote, badger, rabbit, and even skunk.

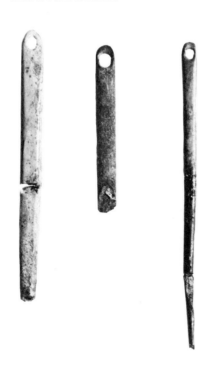

Fine bone needles (shown here somewhat larger than actual size) which date from 9,000 B.P. or earlier have been found in North America only at the Lind Coulee and Marmes sites of Washington and the Hell Gap and Lindemeir sites of Wyoming and Colorado. Such needles may actually have been in widespead use, however; being tiny splinters, they are easily broken and readily subject to disintegration. Lack of archaeological evidence doesn't necessarily mean they did not exist at other locations.

Small gray olivella shells from the Pacific kept appearing down through the layers as far back as 7,000 B.P. Shells of a strictly saltwater snail, they must have come to Palouse Canyon in trade, or possibly from long journeys to the coast via the Snake and Columbia rivers, or overland. Most were drilled, probably to string as necklaces.

At the end of summer 1965 the geologist with the WSU Laboratory of Anthropology, the late Dr. Roald Fryxell, hired a bulldozer to cut a trench from the rock shelter to the floodplain below. He wanted to compare the geologic record there with what he already had worked out for the shelter. In the bottom of the trench, fourteen feet below ground level, lay a startling discovery. It was a concentration of charred bone fragments. Fryxell collected them and took them to Gustafson. Some proved human. The rest were elk. If these bones belonged at that depth they held promise of being much older than anything found so far. If the bulldozer had knocked them into the trench they quite surely held less value.

A search began for proof one way or the other. Whenever they could over nearly a two-year period, Fryxell and Gustafson led classes to Marmes Rockshelter to look for something indisputably in place which would demonstrate where the bone fragments belonged. The Ozette archaeological project over on the coast was underway and time for Marmes was a problem. But finally the needed evidence came. Fryxell found more bone, this time unquestionably belonging fourteen feet below the surface. Gustafson identifed the new pieces, too, as human. He even fit one fragment into a partial skullcap he already had been able to piece together.

Little time remained for archaeology. In eight months the spillway gates at Lower Monumental Dam would close, and two or three days after that water would lap halfway to the ceiling of the rock shelter. Yet here was a chance to add truly early human occupancy to the detailed knowedge of environmental events already reconstructed as far back as the close of the last ice age. The new discovery lay sandwiched in time below the Mazama ash layer of 6,700 B.P. and below river mussel shell carbon dated as at least 9,000 years old, but above Glacier Peak ash from an eruption at about 13,000 B.P.

Most of the claims for discovery of ancient man in America fail scientifically. There simply isn't enough to prove them. The sediments that bones have come from may be so jumbled nobody can decipher the true sequence, or a skull or other find may be removed from the ground but not reported until too late to study its true context. In contrast, the Marmes discovery came after years of patient reconstruction of past events, and it represented part of a long continuum of human occupation at the rock shelter. Radiocarbon dating ultimately gave an age of more than 10,000 years to "Marmes Man." The bones are some of the oldest human remains in the western hemisphere to be documented geologically and environmentally as well as archaeologically. Instead of an isolated find, here was evidence of early man and his tools.

Olivella shells from Marmes Rockshelter were drilled as though for stringing into a necklace.

Work continued in the rock shelter and on the floodplain, with the bulldozer to strip off the top six or eight feet of overburden. Once down to the deposits, excavation depended on hand shovels, trowels, dental picks, and brushes. WSU professors Grover Krantz and the late Henry Irwin joined Daugherty, Fryxell, and Gustafson in the field and the laboratory; a visiting physical anthropologist from Poland, Dr. Tadeuz Bielicki, consulted with them; men from the United States Geological Survey volunteered their expertise; archaeology graduate students joined the crew.

Discoveries came rapidly. Animal bones in the same layer as the human bone had been cracked open for the marrow, and some were burned. Bones from the hindquarters of an elk lay a few feet from vertebrae and ribs, evidently brought here from a hunt. Gustafson's measurements showed this animal as 10 percent larger than a modern elk, apparently a holdover from the late Pleistocene when fauna overall were larger than current fauna. Stone spearpoints were found, somewhat larger and heavier than the arrowheads from the upper layers of the rock shelter. They belonged to the millennia when hunters stalked close enough to jab their points into prey rather than shooting from a distance. Choppers, scrapers, and knives were brushed free of the dusty deposits, documented in place, and recovered. A puzzle was an owl claw found lying between two chips of stone. Evidently the claw and the chips once had been in a hide or woven pouch long since decayed and gone. A hole pierced the bone, perhaps to permit wearing the claw as an amulet.

The human skullcap proved a modern type. Were Marmes Man to return dressed in current fashion he wouldn't be noticed in the checkout line at a supermarket—he or she, for sex stayed the secret of the skull. Grover Krantz, a physical anthropologist could say, however, that the person was in the late teens or early twenties. Sutures—the lines along which a skull fuses—weren't yet fully joined, an aid to determining the age. By late summer, with mere weeks left, two other partial skulls were found. One belonged to a child six or eight years old, as judged from the teeth, the other to a young adult.

This last one, Marmes III, was lifted out still resting in a block of the deposits that had held it through the ten millennia. One of the problems of archaeology is that the process of recovering evidence destroys the very deposits being investigated. Preservation of actual strata such as those holding the Marmes III skull partly offsets the problem. So do detailed records. Nobody can go back to a completed excavation to look again and puzzle over something not previously considered. But they can consult field notes, preserved soil columns and peels, and also scale drawings and photographs of stratigraphy and of archaeological features.

Graduate students made scale drawings sufficiently detailed to include pebbles as small as a half-inch in diameter (top), after geologist Roald Fryxell had traced the individual layers cross-sectioned by pit walls (bottom).

Dr. Henry Irwin, (top, left) brushed preservative onto the Marmes III skullcap as it lay in situ within a block of strata jacketed with plaster of paris preparatory to removal (right). The incomplete fusing of the sutures indicated a young adult (bottom, left).

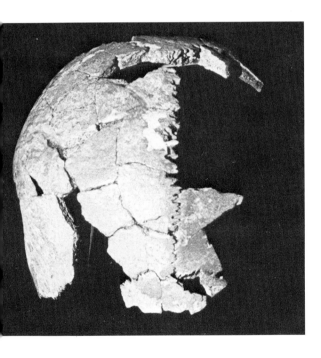

A water screen (above) was used to recover fine plant and animal remains (below). A handful of this material came from a half-inch layer of sediment painstakingly scraped from the floor of a square that measured five feet on a side.
Among the tiny flakes of bone were fossil seeds and a rodent tooth. Since various species of plants require certain conditions to grow, indication of their presence in the past points to the climatic conditions of the time. In a similar way, animals—particularly small species that cannot travel far—also indicate past conditions.

These can be consulted at any time, and their story often is remarkably complete. At the Marmes site every shovelful of earth was screened either by shaking through a one-quarter-inch screen or, where warranted, by washing through a one-sixteenth-inch nylon mesh. The screening was done by excavation square and level so as to record exactly where any finds had originated. Bone needles were found this way in the water screen. There were five of them, splinters so tiny they couldn't have been noticed in any other way. The discovery here came a few years before the similar discovery at Lind Coulee. Even today, such fine needles are known in America from only four sites. The water screen also yielded fossil seeds and miniscule bones and teeth that proved helpful in reconstructing the past plant and animal life of the canyon. This, in turn, suggested the climate since most plants and small animals survive only within a fairly narrow spectrum of temperature and moisture.

One find allowed another, with still more direct evidence concerning the people of 10,000 years ago coming from the rock shelter. Four feet below the Mazama ash and well in front of the present cave overhang was a hearth with bits of bone. It would have been in the old floor of the cave since erosion constantly cuts deeper into the cliff, shifting the opening higher as rocks fall from the ceiling and raise the floor level. In this position students found the hearth with blackened bone and a beautifully made basalt knife blade. Fryxell estimated that 2,000 years or more would be needed to form the depth of rubble between the hearth and the 6,700-year-old ash. That meant the hearth was about the same age as the skull fragments from the floodplain below. Dr. Daugherty determined that it must be a cremation hearth, much the oldest so far known anywhere in the new world, and quite possibly the explanation of the three charred Marmes skulls. Grover Krantz found that the bone fragments belonged to at least five persons—two adults and three children between the ages of eight and fourteen.

Only about one quarter of the floodplain deposits had been excavated and some of the early floors of the rock shelter remained, but time ran out. In order to save the site so that work could continue the Corps of Army Engineers built a levee to hold back the waters of the reservoir. An underlying gravel layer, however, acted as conduit and water rose inside the levee as rapidly as without. No amount of pumping stemmed its flow. The crew draped walls with plastic sheeting and filled the excavations with sand to prevent destruction by slumping in case the reservoir should silt in and make possible resumption of the archaeology. For the time being nothing more could be done. February 1969 not only was bitterly cold, it was doleful for the WSU team: the site with all of its remaining evidence lay drowned.

That particular search for the oldest man in America had ended. Even so it stands as a landmark not only for the knowledge it gave of early man and his environment, but also for its role in quickening public awareness of our long cultural past on this continent. The race against time had gained congressional support and even White House attention. It had helped influence passage of legislation intended to safeguard the fragile evidence of the past and make it a known part of our common heritage.

Marmes floodplain excavations as seen from the rock shelter. When the site had to be abandoned to the rising water of Lower Monumental Reservoir, excavation squares were draped with plastic sheeting and backfilled with gravel to prevent slumping. This was a protective measure in case future conditions permit resumption of the archaeology.

At the Marmes site, bones of an elk 10 percent larger than those alive today are drawn to scale, part of the documentation (left). An owl's claw sandwiched between flakes of stone lay in deposits 10,000 years old (below).

Opposite: A paper "fence diagram" of excavation squares (above, left) and a scale model of the rock shelter (above, right) provided three-dimensional visualization of deposits even after the site was flooded. As part of the process of dating organic material by the radiocarbon method, methane is collected from samples by freezing it with liquid nitrogen at about $-320°F$ (below). The amount of carbon-14 within the methane is then counted to determine the age of the sample at the time of death. This is possible because that particular isotope of carbon, which is absorbed from the atmosphere by living plants and animals, begins to disintegrate as soon as death occurs. The breakdown takes place at a fixed rate that can be measured and converted into elapsed time.

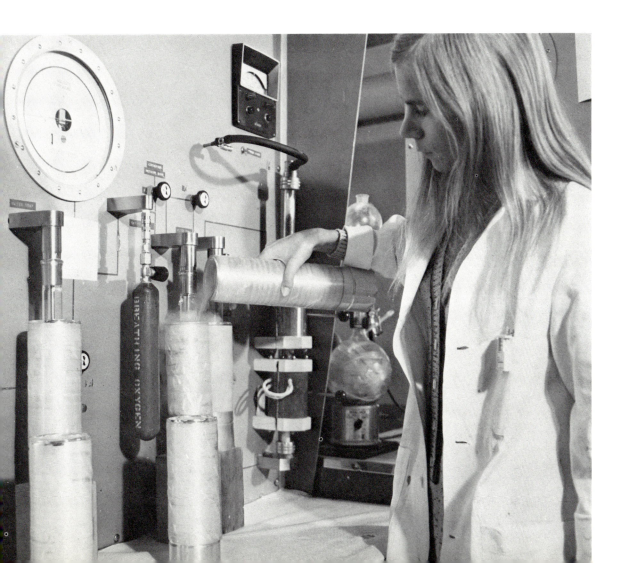

Northwest Adaptations

Since at least 9,000 B.P. salmon, preyed upon by man and basic to his adaptation, have been a part of the Northwest skein of life. Their vertebrae have been found in archaeological deposits nine thousand years old at The Dalles on the lower Columbia River, and at Kettle Falls on the upper Columbia, where evidence of summertime occupation of an island strongly suggests fishing.

Migration from natal waters to the ocean and back again is comparable to the migration of ducks and geese, or of elk and caribou, in the sense that they all migrate as a means of coping with seasonally adverse environments. Northern rivers get so cold in winter that their food supply would be far too limited to support the hordes of mature salmon that come to spawn; and adult salmon feed in the rich pastures of the ocean, not in the rivers. On the other hand, rivers are ideal for reproduction. The ample oxygen held by cold water enhances development of eggs and newly hatched fish, and the small food supply suffices. Migration allows the best of two worlds: riverine conditions for the young, marine conditions for the adults.

The five salmon species of the Northwest depend on precise conditions at the redds. Sockeye spawn mostly in lakes, especially where ground water seeps through shore gravels and holds temperature more constant than is generally true for lake water. Pinks and chums get along where water level and temperature fluctuate, for these species migrate soon after hatching and since their spawning grounds are near river mouths they have only a short journey to the ocean. Chinook and coho spend from one to three years in fresh water before entering the ocean, so they need rivers with fairly stable conditions. Usually these are long and large enough to equalize effects such as locally heavy rain and runoff, or extreme heat or cold.

Development of optimum conditions for spawning varies by mere days from year to year, with no two species duplicating each other's requirements. This served man's needs well. Salmon offered a food resource that was predictable, run after run entering the rivers, those having the farthest to go coming first, others following. No husbandry was needed, only catching and storing.

How long before 9,000 B.P. these processes began isn't known. Certainly the floods of late Pleistocene time would have destroyed all redds in their paths. Also, because of suspended silt, glacial meltwater across northern Washington probably meant no salmon spawned there until sometime after 13,000 B.P. Silt smothers developing eggs, clogs the hiding places within the gravel needed by tiny hatchlings, and abrades the gills. Lower reaches of the Columbia and its tributaries may have been suitable during most of the ice age, however.

Salmon have been used by Northwest man for at least 9,000 years, for their bones are found in deposits of that age. Absence of the bones is difficult to evaluate. It may mean that people were not fishing at that locality; or it may reflect a reverential attitude toward salmon which required a ritual disposal of the bones. This is true of the widely practiced First Salmon Ceremony still observed in some villages. It also may have been true in the ancient past. The best dip net locations (opposite and above) were—and are—at eddies and at constrictions of a river's flow.

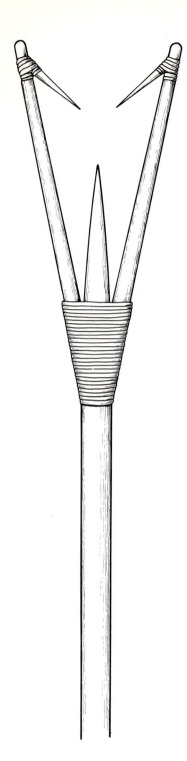

Volcanic ash that washed into rivers from sporadic eruptions perhaps occasionally polluted water beyond the mechanical or chemical tolerance of fish. Landslides and droughts must have disrupted runs. In some cases salmon may have reestablished their redds in only a decade or two; in others fifty years or more probably passed. Streams newly free of glacial ice in Alaska today give a chance to observe the initial establishment of fish runs, and comparable data on recovery rates following major landslides comes from the 1913 disaster at Hell's Gate on the Fraser River, British Columbia. The sockeye catch there immediately dropped by 80 percent, and fifty years later it had rebuilt to only half its pre-slide level.

Aboriginal man must have experienced such disruptions of the salmon runs, but even a small percentage of successfully returning fish would keep alive fishing techniques and ceremonies. A man might lose the chance to teach skills to a young son, but probably he could teach them to his grandson. Successive generations didn't have to redevelop techniques; they drew on the accumulated knowledge of predecessors.

What equipment the earliest fishermen used isn't known. The fish vertebrae at The Dalles point to successful fishing, but not to the method used. Similarly, at Kettle Falls there could be little reason to camp on Hayes Island except to fish, although seven river cobbles notched on each side as though for net sinkers are the only seemingly direct evidence of fishing. Projectile points from that time have not been found there, nor have there been animal bones with butchering marks—indications of hunting camps. Cobble choppers and scrapers may have been used for woodworking. Possibly men cut stakes and pounded them upright to support nets or secured platforms to canyon walls for dip netting or spearing fish at the rapids.

Through the millennia fishermen developed a wide variety of superbly designed and manufactured gear. Probably the simplest worked as effectively as that which seems more complex, however, with different sorts of gear, much of it ingenious, suiting different situations. For example, leisters provided multiple points set opposing one another. A thrashing fish couldn't dislodge itself; and since the barbs angled upward, there was little risk of breaking their tips against rocky stream bottoms. Harpoons with detachable heads exhibit another kind of excellence. The shaft let a man thrust or hurl his weapon accurately but, once the blade had penetrated, the entire head separated from the shaft and was held by an attached line. This permitted retrieval of the fish more readily than a shaft could because anything rigid would tend to snap as the heavy fish struggled. Smooth bone points from the 9,000 B.P. level of The Dalles deposits may be from leisters or harpoons, and the pieces of notched bone found at Lind Coulee also could be from some sort of fishing gear.

Their points angling in from three directions, leisters provided a fairly sure means of holding a struggling fish. Points were of bone or of antler. Lashings were usually of cherry bark, ideal because it is tough, resists rot, and shrinks when wet, thus tightening into place whatever it is binding.

Hand-held dip nets, gill nets, and a variety of other specialized nets facilitated efficient fishing. So did stone walls built to obstruct rivers and divert fish into traps or to locations convenient for spearing; but these leave little archaeological evidence. Wood and fiber decay quickly. Flowing water destroys unmaintained walls or traps, even of stone. Yet these devices helped to concentrate the catch and to some extent worked for a man while he himself was off doing other things. Early missionaries' journals tell of seven to eight hundred salmon a day taken at Nez Perce weirs. Left open most of the time, these frameworks of poles and wattle didn't stop fish from getting up river to the spawning grounds or keep other villages from getting a share of the runs. Leaving them open also prevented river debris from piling up against them to the point that water pressure might be destructive.

Estimates place the annual catch of salmon at about 123 million pounds by historic times—about a pound per day per person. Probably this heavy reliance on fishing developed as population grew. Certainly in many parts of the world it seems to have been the need for more food that prompted development of agriculture and of herding; in the Northwest the salmon runs amounted to a nutritional reservoir already waiting. Furthermore, salmon were far from the only fish used. Rainbow trout, cutthroat, steelhead, sturgeon, whitefish, and a host of others served as food, each recognized as a distinct type and called by its own name.

People on both sides of the mountains built weirs to concentrate into one area fish swimming upstream. Sometimes holes in a lattice-work fence set crosswise to the stream led salmon into traps, or to where fishermen waited with dip nets or spears. Weirs across major salmon rivers were owned communally, at least by historic times, and everyone shared in the catch. On small streams they might be individually owned. Worn stakes still stand in a few Northwest streams and estuaries, mute testimony to weirs long-since abandoned.

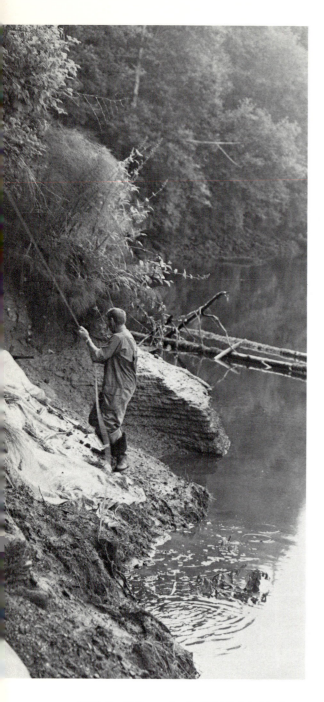

Many fishing methods involved group cooperation. One person alone can't build and operate a weir on a major river. And since most weirs didn't last from one season to the next, their presence meant not just occasional cooperation but regularized, repeated cooperation year after year. Furthermore, catching hundreds of fish is pointless unless they can be preserved and stored for later use. Without storage, a population is limited to the carrying capacity of the season that produces the least amount of food, generally winter. With storage, the season of food processing offers sustenance for use during the period of low productivity.

Large-scale fishing and storage dictated a yearly period of settled life and determined its location, generally at river constrictions where fish congregate. It also involved not just building and operating a weir or trap or seine—and platforms for dipping or gaffing—but also building drying racks, sun shades, and smokehouses, and making baskets and boxes, and having enough sharp knives on hand to cut the fish and score the flesh for efficient processing. The labor force had to be organized. That, in turn, may well have fostered development of more complex social organization.

Unlike the product of most hunts, successful fishing meant tons of meat to process—immediately. Washington State University archaeologist Randall Schalk even speculates that effective handling of anadromous fish runs constitutes a primary reason for increasingly rigid social organization from south to north along the coast. Optimum spawning conditions fall within an ever-narrowing period to the north, the runs of fish overlapping the availability of other vital resources. This increases the need for efficient handling of the fleeting largesse. People perform specialized tasks, dividing up the labor; and this creates a need to redistribute the results. To achieve that, authoritative leadership and codified patterns of conduct are needed. Rank, class, and clan develop. So does a sense of stewardship toward stored food and toward areas of abundant resources. These characteristics are particularly pronounced along the coasts of northern British Columbia and southeastern Alaska, where spawning runs are the most concentrated.

With the Hoko work schedule dictated by low-tide exposure of river mouth deposits, an archaeologist rappelled over the bank to excavate a section where no other foothold was feasible (above). A sandstone rock lay in the Hoko deposits still held by the fiber knot that once had secured it to a split-root gill net. The stone itself is unmodified and could not be recognized as an artifact except for the knot (right).

Of course along the coast, fishing wasn't restricted to rivers and lakes. Men evidently caught cod and halibut and other marine species at least as early as 2,750 B.P., for specialized hooks quite surely used for these fish have come from stratified deposits at Hoko River, on the Olympic Peninsula east of Neah Bay. The hooks are similar to those used by Indians in historic times, and the metal halibut hook used by today's commercial fishermen is shaped like the steamed and bent wooden hook of the past. Only the remarkable preservation in constantly damp sediments is permitting recovery of the truly ancient wooden fish gear. Ordinarily such material decays within mere decades but, at Hoko, archaeologists directed by Dr. Dale Croes of Washington State University have found scores of wooden leister and harpoon points, as well as fishhooks. To the delight of Makah Indians, who have fished the Hoko from time immemorial, the mud even held a gill net knotted of split cedar roots. It lay in a tangle, still tied to a sandstone weight.

Dr. Dale Croes gently freed a burden basket probably used for carrying fish to camp. Ninety percent of the artifacts found at Hoko are made of wood, which at most sites is lost to decay. This high percentage of ordinarily perishable material indicates the difficulty of fully understanding past material cultures from remaining stone, bone, and shell artifacts, the materials likely to withstand the ravages of time.

The 2,700-year-old knives found at Hoko River (top, left) were replicated and tested in use, including the cutting of fish (top, right). Steamed and bent wooden hooks from Hoko deposits (center, left) resemble those used within historic times by Makah Indians fishing for halibut, such as were photographed on the Neah Bay beach around the turn of the century (lower). The hooks as well as bones of various types of bottom fish indicate the presence of seaworthy watercraft.

The rare discovery of such equipment thousands of years old acts as a reminder of what a small percentage of past culture most archaeological sites reveal. Finding evidence of a speared mastodon, or of butchered elk and bison doesn't mean that ancient hunters subsisted on a meat diet—only that at the particular location hunting was one of man's activities. Salmon vertebrae, or halibut hooks, don't mean people lived by fishing alone. On the contrary, the food base was broader than physical evidence can show and, although inferences can be drawn from archaeological excavations, the past really is no more than glimpsed. The pigments found at Lind Coulee, for instance, suggest artistry; but what kind? Cosmetic? Painting on hide or wood? No evidence of the art remains.

The Hoko artifacts lie at the river mouth covered by sediments deposited as the bar slowly moved seaward. For Makahs today this has been a chum salmon station and, judging from the recovered archaeological material, it also was a fishing camp nearly three thousand years ago. Occupation must have been in fall—the time of the chum runs, which are the last of the year—for spruce and hemlock cones with their scales open as though to release seeds are common in the deposits. The fishing gear is present. So are sturdy baskets most likely for carrying fish back to camp, and knives probably used in processing the catch.

The knives are of particular interest to archaeologists. There are six: stone blades about the size of a man's thumbnail are sandwiched between five-inch splints of red cedar and bound with strips of cedar bark or spruce root. Similar stone tools have come from dozens of other Northwest sites dating from 9,000 to 1,500 B.P. But these are the first to be found still hafted. Jeff Flenniken, a Washington State University archaeologist, made exact copies of the Hoko knives and tested them in preparing basketry materials, working with wood, and cutting fish. For the basketry and woodworking the knives proved poor tools; furthermore, wear marks left on replicated blades didn't match those on the ancient blades. For gutting and filleting fish, however, they worked splendidly.

Makahs apparently have been roasting salmon beside open fires (left) in much the same way for the last several centuries. Split sticks identical with those used today have come from buried houses at Ozette, which date to 450 B.P. (above).

Most of American archaeology is based largely on remnant stone tools; evidence comes from stone, since wood and fiber usually are gone. Hoko River and a few other wet sites are exceptions, but anywhere in the world nearly all we can know of mankind—from the earliest dawn of culture to recent centuries—depends on stone. Writing didn't develop until about five thousand years ago, and because of both rarity and poor preservation few truly early manuscripts exist. Oral tradition dies out. Stone remains the key to the past—and this gives great value to intensive studies such as Flenniken's and earlier pioneering replication by Don Crabtree of Idaho State University Museum.

Stone tools as a whole are far from primitive, if the term connotes marginal usefulness or outright inferiority. A stone axe, for example, takes only three or four hours to make, depending on materials and methods, and in less than a minute it can cut a two-inch pine; in eight to ten minutes it can chop through a tree the diameter of a man's thigh. Flenniken, testing a replicated basalt axe, needed 1,457 strokes to fell a four-inch willow and another 70 to sever it from its stump. He found the axe had to bite in all around the trunk, rather than coming on one side only, first from above then from below, as is usual when using a steel axe.

Skill in making and using stone tools often began with the getting of raw material. Some stone could be picked up on the surface or pried loose easily; some had to be quarried. From a quarrying experiment, Crabtree reports getting only one or two blocks of useable stone after hours of work using aboriginal methods. Tools of a hard stone such as chert or certain types of basalt work best. They induce great shock with minimum velocity, important for removing large flakes from a ground mass or for roughing blanks into forms ready for final shaping. This last careful flaking or chipping requires a tool of relatively soft stone, or of antler, horn, or bone. Such a material allows precise control in the removal of flakes and avoids bruising and weakening the stone.

Some types of stone, such as obsidian and agate flake easily in their natural state. Other, more coarsely textured stones, such as most chert, flint, and jasper, need to be heat-treated before they respond well to flaking. Crabtree found he could get only half-inch flakes off an untreated flint core compared to two-inch flakes from the same stone after heat-treating. Electron microscope examination shows that heating drives out moisture and causes recrystallization. This produces a finer texture, which allows the stone to break to a sharper edge.

Arrowheads (shown here actual size) did not need to be as large as spearpoints in order to achieve the same results since they struck with greater force.

Aboriginal man had both expertise and finesse in his heat technology. Too much heat may explode stone or reduce tensile strength. Sudden raising or lowering of temperature causes crazing. Furthermore, each kind of stone reacts differently. To assure control, stoneworkers used special fire pits intended specifically for heat-treating, not for general cooking or warming. These only are beginning to be recognized archaeologically. From bottom to top such pits were layered with coals, sand, the stone being treated, more sand, more coals, and a final capping of sand. At least among Australian aborigines today the whole process of heat treating may take as long as four days, with frequent attention and adjustment.

Much as fishing equipment evolved from simple spears to more elaborate devices, so weapons for hunting land animals also changed with time. First probably were spears such as the bone-tipped one found with the Manis mastodon, or simple stone-tipped spears. Best evidence is that early hunters thrust or threw their spears, often after having stampeded herd animals like bison and elk past men lying in ambush, or having driven massive prey like a mammoth or mastodon into soft mud where it would mire and become more safely approachable.

Next in the developmental sequence came the atlatl, a simple device for throwing spears or darts with greater force than by hand and arm alone. In principle this amounted simply to an extension of the arm, letting a man hurl a spear twice as far as otherwise was possible. Furthermore, the spear traveled faster and so hit with greater shock and penetration, important in successful hunting. The spearpoint imbedded in the Manis mastodon rib probably was thrown with an atlatl, judging from how deeply it penetrated the animal. Certainly by 8,500 B.P. men were using this technique, for an atlatl spur came from Five Mile Rapids near The Dalles dating from that age.

Overall, atlatls had largely given way to the bow and arrow by about 3,500 B.P., but the process was a slow one rather than a revolutionary change. Even so, the bow and arrow differed greatly from its predecessors. Arrows traveled farther than spears, their propulsion coming from a new source: a string held under tension, then released.

Manufacturing stone tools involved much more than the random hitting of one rock with another. Direct percussion (left) sufficed to sharpen an edge on river cobbles, resulting in effective tools which were used from earliest times into recent centuries. Pressure flaking (right), using a resilient material such as antler, provided more control for shaping tools from roughed-out blanks. Other common techniques included indirect percussion—striking a punch with a hammerstone instead of hitting the tool blank itself—and grinding, sawing, incising, and pecking.

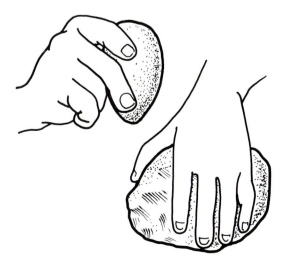

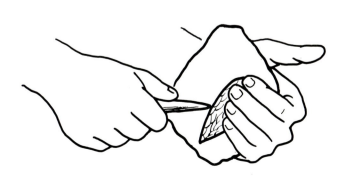

Oddly enough, the real skill in making a bow and arrow wasn't flaking the arrowhead, but getting the shaft straight. Some historic accounts say that anybody could flake a satisfactory arrowhead but only specialists produced straight shafts. Often a short separate section joined an arrowhead to the shaft proper. Breakage was intended to occur there, allowing salvage of the shaft proper, which was the slow difficult part of the arrow to replace. Bows needed to have only thirty to forty-five pounds of pull in order to shoot 250 yards. An arrowhead's size was related to the size of the bow and to personal preference as well as to the size, weight, and balance of the arrow as a whole. Stone penetrated so well that large arrowheads weren't necessarily needed even for bison or elk.

Stone tools often reveal ingenious workmanship when examined closely. Consider for instance scrapers found at Lind Coulee. Little more than an inch or two across, these are flaked at one end to produce a curved blade that is sharpened only on one edge. Turned over, the flat "handle" end also is sharpened on one edge: held one way the tool offered a curved edge; flipped, there was a straight edge.

As further illustration of the exacting suitability of stone tools for their intended tasks, visualize the process of extracting marrow. Batter a bone with a cobble straight from the river bar, and the hammer will slide off. Hit harder, and the bone will mash down into the marrow. But knock a few flakes off one side of the cobble to produce a jagged edge, then lay the bone on top of a second stone as anvil. Now strike, and the bone will crack open neatly and reveal a thick roll of marrow. Go a step further and ask contemporary Indians what they remember of such processes: for instance, at the mouth of the Hoh River on the Olympic Peninsula, Quileute people speak of a face cream made by boiling elk marrow. With the addition of red pigment it became rouge. Used plain it protected against chapping when out in a canoe or digging clams.

Stone pestles (above) were made by pecking and grinding. They were used for a variety of pounding and grinding purposes including preparation of berries, roots, and meat. Basalt (right), readily available on both sides of the Cascade Mountains, was commonly used for tools.

From such inferences even simple stone tools take on immediacy. Or sometimes their sheer excellence speaks for itself. Obsidian blades, for example, are many times sharper than surgical steel scalpels or Platinum-plus razor blades. Poured from the throats of volcanoes as glass, this stone cools before crystals form and therefore it can be flaked in any direction and will break to an edge literally one molecule thick. Don Crabtree three times has been faced with major surgery—including removal of a lung—and has convinced his doctor to operate with obsidian knives. Despite incisions nearly a foot and a half long, only the stitches have left noticeable scars. The incision itself has healed essentially without a mark. Obsidian is so sharp it seems to cut without crushing cells. It almost is too sharp; the tendency is to overcut. Special hafting—and experience—are needed to control the blade, and with its extreme thinness the edge breaks easily. Even so, the use of obsidian knives, particularly in cosmetic surgery, holds some promise.

The approach of modern archaeology always has been more than simply digging "things" out of the ground, and increasingly it has become a compound of multiple insights. Detailed studies such as Crabtree's and Flenniken's are a part of this. So are reconstructions of past environment, for the culture of any particular time can be understood only in relation to its environment, as we moderns facing depleted energy sources and accelerated pollution are suddenly aware. Man doesn't live apart. He belongs to a whole, and that whole keeps changing according to various factors. Understanding what they have been through time comes from techniques as esoteric as the study of oxygen isotopes in substances such as tree rings and glacial ice. This indicates past climate because oxygen, as other elements, has several forms and the ratio of one to another varies with temperature.

A finely made basalt knife (right) lay within a 10,000-year-old cremation hearth at Marmes Rockshelter. Wafer-thin microblades found at Ryegrass Coulee, near Vantage, date from about 6,600 B.P. (below). They seem to represent the extension onto the Columbia Plateau of a technology that can be traced back through time to the Arctic and Eurasia. This method of comparing distinctive types of stone tools is a basic technique used by archaeologists in understanding past cultural patterns. How microblades were hafted or used isn't known. They are shown here at about actual size—tiny slivers that rest lightly in the hand.

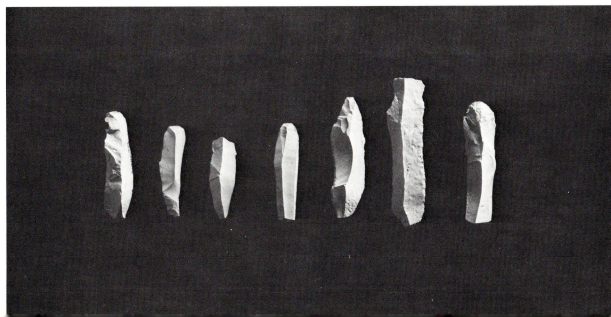

Remarkably detailed understanding comes, too, from studies such as the relation between volcanic ash and pollen. For example, Mazama ash first fell in Idaho's Bitterroot Mountains in autumn. Additional ash fell the following spring, and also during the next two years. These ashfalls suppressed certain types of lake growth, as indicated by some algae, whereas the growth of others, such as diatoms, was stimulated. Terrestrial species were benefitted, perhaps because the ash acted as a mulch and held in soil moisture. Varying results of this sort obviously must have affected man far beyond the initial dustiness of the ash itself.

Aside from environmental changes caused by climate shifts and rare catastrophic events, the land itself changes through geomorphic processes rapid enough to register within a human lifetime. River deltas furnish an example. Before diking and channeling, the Skagit delta built seaward a probable ten to twenty feet a year, and although the rate in the distant past can't be known, it may well have been about the same. Sites once coastal lie inland now, and former islands rise as hills surrounded by pasture, not water.

What tools and methods man might best use for hunting game, catching fish, or digging roots depended on the particular conditions of the time—and these depended on a host of interacting factors. For instance, climate and soil affect what plants can grow; plants determine where herbivores can live; the presence of herbivores dictates that of carnivores; and so on. Climate in many ways is a key. In Washington, conditions have gone from cool temperatures for the first several thousand years following retreat of the continental ice sheets to a period from perhaps 7,500 to 4,500 B.P. that was warmer and drier than at present, and finally to the moderating of our present climate. Along the coast temperatures have varied less than inland, owing to the ameliorating effect of the ocean.

At the height of the altithermal, as the warm period is called, western Washington Julys may have averaged about 5° F. warmer than they were soon after the last ice age, and are now. Overall, vegetation evolved from a parkland of lodgepole pine, to alder and Douglas-fir, and on to the western hemlock dominant at present. Precisely what happened, and where, of course varied. In the rain shadow of the Olympic Mountains, including parts of Puget Sound and the San Juan and Gulf islands, oak and madrona extended their range during the altithermal; deer found ideal habitat; and bulbs important in human diet, such as camas and onion, multiplied.

In eastern Washington the post-glacial cool climate is shown by evidence that includes an arctic fox jaw found in floodplain deposits at Marmes Rockshelter and clear differences in the rates of rockfall within the cave itself. During excavation archaeologists found the post-glacial chill was reflected in a greater amount of rockfall in the lower layers of the deposits, compared to that in overlying layers. Ice in ceiling cracks had pried loose blocks. Then when climate warmed, less ice formed and there was less rockfall. Pollen sequences from eastern Washington point to cold steppe vegetation following ice withdrawal, then a spruce-pine forest, followed by an increase in grasses and composites, and finally the pines, grasses, and sagebrush of today.

Lakes obviously dried as the ice age waned. Plants available as food and for raw materials changed. Animal species came and went. Man adapted, mingling evidence of his presence with that of the changing environment.

Estuaries and bays afforded flat village areas, quiet waters for easy canoeing, and varied food resources. The Skagit Delta west from Mount Vernon (above); midden in an excavation wall at the Minard site, Grays Harbor, and stone and bone artifacts found there (left and below).

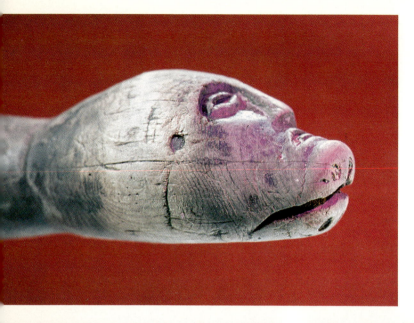

With continuous year-round operation since 1970, the excavation of houses at Ozette buried 450 years ago by mudflow has produced more than 42,000 artifacts. These include objects of wood and fiber ordinarily lost to decay. Examples are a club carved to represent a seal when viewed from the side and a man's face when viewed from above (top left); a stylized human form (below left); and a whale ornamenting the handle of a weaving implement (below right). Bone carvings include a two-inch man found crouched within a mussel shell (bottom right).

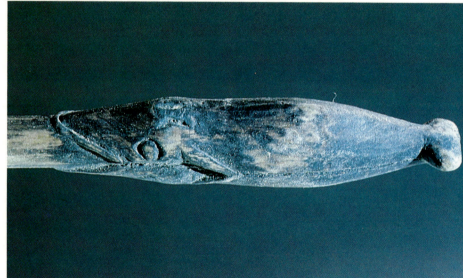

Ozette Village (above) is located on the roadless outer coast of the Olympic Peninsula. A wooden club carved with an owl's head (right) lies on a house floor beside a canoe paddle, bits of cordage, a bow, and parts of a loom. Archaeologists excavate with water sprayed from hoses (below left). The artifacts recovered include finely carved clubs (below right) such as this one, probably used ceremonially.

Along the Strait of Juan de Fuca east of Neah Bay is the mouth of the Hoko River, an Indian fishing station for at least 2,500 years. Riverbank deposits hold fiber nets, wooden fishhooks, and other usually perishable materials. Archaeologists wash them free using water pumped from the river (above left and right). A stone knife still hafted in a five-inch cedar handle lies in the deposits (opposite). Many wooden fishhooks with fiber lanyards (opposite, bottom left) have been recovered, as have basket fragments (below right). Indian-smoked smelt today probably are of the type once prepared here (opposite bottom right).

Natural shelters at the base of basalt cliffs along the rivers and coulees of eastern Washington have served man as campsites and for storage from earliest times. Porcupine Cave along the Palouse River (above, interior and exterior) is typical. Pictographs (painted designs) and petroglyphs (pecked designs) are frequent on rocks above water courses. Known in Washington are 185 such sites including those at Little Klickitat River (opposite, top), on the Colville Reservation (opposite, bottom left) and along the lower Columbia (opposite, bottom right).

Palouse River Canyon upriver from Marmes Rockshelter.

The Columbia Plateau

On the Snake River about forty miles southeast of Lind Coulee is a basalt cliff half a mile long, nondescript except for a series of nine rock shelters at its base. These are the Windust Caves, excavated during the summers of 1959 to 1961 by Harvey Rice of Washington State University.

Five of the caves lay choked with talus and basalt rubble dislodged during construction of the Northern Pacific Railroad branch line. Amateur collectors had churned the deposits in three of four remaining caves, leaving a chaos of pits and back-dirt piles. Even so, one of these caves yielded a sequence of material that gave archaeologists one of their earliest looks at remnants of Columbia Plateau culture from nine thousand years ago into the present. Artifacts from all of this time span were found in layers one above the other.

Ironically, it was railroad rubble fallen into the cave that kept the collectors from churning the deposits with the valuable sequence. The archaeology crew spent three weeks with picks and shovels clearing this mound of rock debris, and under it they found stratified deposits with no sign of disturbance. Excavation posed problems. The cave extended back seventy feet but was only twelve feet wide. Bedrock lay more than twenty feet under the top of the railroad rubble, itself eight feet thick. This meant working in a pit, winching dirt up by the bucketful. As depth increased, natural light dwindled so markedly that at first aluminum foil reflectors were improvised to spot sunlight back into the cave, and later generator-powered lights were rigged. Dust was constant. Worse still, collectors persisted in rummaging about in the cave during the months between field seasons. In the winter of 1960–61 they utterly destroyed the ten-foot section of stratified deposits scheduled for excavation in the final summer before the flooding of the reservoir behind Ice Harbor Dam.

Nonetheless, projectile points and other artifacts were recovered in an unbroken sequence that dated from the end of the post-glacial period into the present. What may have been lost to vandalism never will be known, though undoubtedly detail forever is missing from the record. Even were the pilfered objects to be turned in they would be of little value, for archaeological documentation rests on the study of artifacts *in situ*, that is, lying in place undisturbed. It deals with relationships as much as with objects.

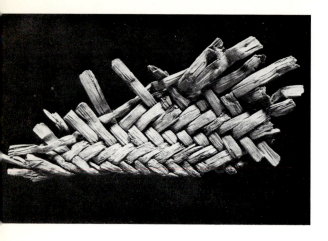

From what was present, however, Rice concluded that through the millennia small hunting bands must have used the cave for temporary shelter. Projectile points lay within the deposits as time markers valuable in themselves, and even more so for comparison with other sites, few of which have more than limited time periods represented. Choppers, scrapers, drills, knives, and other stone tools, as well as the projectile points, came from the cave, but attention was focused on the points. Arranged by age, they show a progression in form and manufacturing technique, not necessarily an improvement through time—for early workmanship was as good as what came later—but a definite and ordered change. Bases of the points changed more than tips; also, points became generally smaller from early millennia to historic times, reflecting the change in weaponry from spears that were thrust to those thrown with atlatls, and finally to bows and arrows. At the time of the excavations, the Windust sequence spanned more time than that of any other single Plateau site. A few years later the Marmes sequence proved equally long and valuable.

The Snake River (below), named for its twisting character, afforded riverine resources such as fish and waterfowl in close proximity to upland resources, including berries and roots. Squirt Cave deposits about 2,000 years old held basketry fragments (above and opposite), a hafted knife (opposite, lower left), and a spool of cordage (opposite, lower right).

Projectile points are common finds throughout Washington. Interestingly, those from the earliest times to perhaps six thousand years ago show great similarity regardless of locale. David Munsell, working mostly west of the Cascade Range, and Frank Leonhardy, working on the Plateau, combined slides and artifacts from their excavations for a lecture and found that although they of course could sort them because of personal familiarity and catalog numbers, there were no differences in style within the collections. This suggests that human adaptation followed essentially the same pattern on both sides of the mountains during this early time—and despite environmental differences east and west, major food resources are the same. Both sides of the state are rich in camas and wapato roots, deer and elk, and salmon. Eventually people began to adapt specifically to whatever environment they occupied, and along the coast there was an increase in fishing, in gathering shellfish, and in hunting sea mammals. Inland, river resources became increasingly utilized. At Kettle Falls excavations directed by University of Idaho archaeologist David Chance indicate that although people were fishing as far back as nine thousand years ago, they seem to have been eating their limited catch on the spot rather than filleting and drying it for storage.

Sound inferences of course are difficult. For example, milling stones point to the use of plant foods—roots pulverized and pounded, hard seedcoats cracked open, and so on—yet the first such stones to appear in the archaeological record don't represent the earliest time plant foods were eaten as a main part of the diet. On the contrary, at least among hunting peoples today (except for those in the Arctic where plant foods are virtually unobtainable), meat provides only around one-third of the annual caloric intake. Most energy requirements are supplied by plant foods. On the Plateau, milling stones seem rare until the altithermal, but roots, berries, and greens must have been major foods long before then. Milling stones and a quantity of chokecherry pits found in the earliest levels of the Marmes deposits bear this out. Furthermore wooden mortars probably were used to process plant foods, though they long since have been lost to decay.

In a similar way finding bone harpoon points or fishhooks—or not finding them—can't be counted on as complete evidence regarding fishing. They say nothing about the possibility of nets or weirs once having been present, or of people perhaps having used wooden fishhooks. Wood and fiber usually decay quickly, leaving no evidence.

Even stone projectile points can be misleading. A point may seem to have tipped a spear or an arrow, yet at Squirt Cave on the Snake River Washington State University archaeologist John Combes found one of the early-style willow leaf points that obviously was not a projectile point but a knife: it still was hafted. Preservation seldom permits this kind of look at the past, and Squirt Cave's deposits go back no more than two thousand years. From stone alone, actual use can best be judged by the type of study in which Jeff Flenniken is specializing. Replicate the artifact, use it in various ways, then match the resulting wear patterns against those of the original.

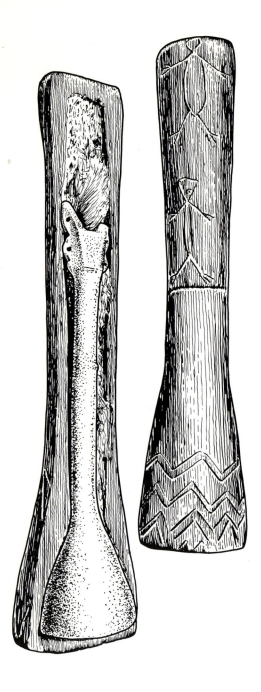

A beautifully fashioned stone pipe was found at Moses Coulee still resting in a carved cedar case padded with shredded bark.

During the warming of the altithermal, life in eastern Washington must have continued the pattern begun earlier. Man is mobile. Let a pine forest dry to grassland, or a grassland to sagebrush, and man doesn't remain rooted. He moves. Higher elevations stay relatively cool and moist; the favorable zone simply climbs a bit. In the lowlands, rivers continue to flow; and if some dry and are gone the diminished flow of others has advantages in facilitating, for example, the harvesting of freshwater mussels.

Foraging societies, practically by definition, exhibit flexibility in their make up. They are broadly based, readily capable of adapting. Hunting furnishes an example of this. The mammoths and mastodons known across the state until perhaps eight thousand years ago died out. Bison vanished, then two thousand years ago returned only to vanish again by early historic times. Man preyed on whatever species were available. Intimate knowledge of animal behavior, and of topography, could be reapplied to make good on any hunting opportunity.

Probably dogs went along on hunts from the time men first wandered onto the Plateau. Bones of two distinct sizes of dogs have come from Jaguar Cave, Idaho in deposits dated at 10,000 B.P. They clearly are not wolf or coyote. Indian dogs had been supposed small, gradually increasing in size through time. But finding large and small dogs already together ten thousand years ago indicates that domestication long since had taken place. There is no direct evidence, but probably the dogs were helping to hunt. The reasons would be the same then as now: man and dog hunt well together. Both enjoy it. And the teamwork is effective whether the quarry is bison or pronghorn, rabbits or ducks.

Foraging groups tend to have more leisure than other forms of society. The whole of the environment serves as combination vegetable garden, feeder lot, and warehouse of materials. Such groups are spared the intensive work demanded of agriculturists by seasons of sowing and harvesting, and the constant attention to husbandry that herds and flocks require. Studies of today's Bushmen of South Africa, for example, show that adults work only two or three days a week to provide themselves with needed food and materials. Furthermore, young people aren't expected to contribute until after they marry, and the percentage of aged who must be supported by the more able-bodied is about the same as in modern industrialized society. Obviously, the concept of an unremitting struggle to survive doesn't characterize today's hunting lifestyle, as had been supposed, and it quite likely wasn't true in the past either.

Cultural change on the Plateau proceeded at a modest pace through the millennia to historic times. New stoneworking technologies appeared from time to time but with no indications of wholesale invasion from without either by people or by ideas. Ground adze blades of nephrite and serpentine stand out among new acquisitions, partly because they suggest woodworking and also because, with British Columbia the nearest source of the stone, they indicate trade. The olivella shells found at Marmes and at various other sites indicate trade with the coast as well.

Interest in life qualities beyond the utilitarian is apparent from carved mussel shell from the Okanogan which must have been for personal adornment or some form of ritual. At The Dalles, bones from cormorants, geese, vultures, condors, and eagles found in lower levels probably indicate some hunting for feathers. The owl claw from the Marmes floodplain also is evidence that people were using birds in ways other than for food. Decorated pipes of steatite and siltstone from the Okanogan region date back at least six thousand years. Life was more than a ceaseless round of subsistence activities.

What kind of dwellings Plateau people lived in for the first several thousand years, aside from rock shelters, isn't known. The earliest indication of a house found so far is at Alpowa, on the Snake River west of Clarkston. This is a pit dating from about five thousand years ago, at the time of occupancy quite surely covered by a superstructure of poles, brush, and mats.

Such pithouses, as they are called, seem to have become increasingly numerous through time, with people living together in villages through the winter, surviving on stored food. The houses were far from being grubby holes in the ground. Indian peoples' memories, ethnographic reports, and archaeological investigation at sites such as Three Springs Bar, Sunset Creek, on the Okanogan Highlands, at Kettle Falls, and a score of other places, reveal quite the opposite. The architecture was ingenious, the accommodation practical and comfortable. In the north, pits dug three or four feet into the ground provided winter warmth, summer coolness. Pole frameworks surrounding these sunken floors were covered with mats, or brush and grass, then banked with a thick insulating layer of earth. On the southern Plateau pits generally weren't quite so deep, and the mats served as coverings for the framework, banked with earth only at the base. A single layer of mats gave shade in summer and kept out wind and showers; they offered ample ventilation when raised at the bottom. In winter multiple layers of mats insulated against the cold, remarkably efficient because they swelled in the dampness and froze, becoming weathertight. Spring and summer dried the mats again and they shrank, giving the airy coolness that makes the ramadas and wickiups of desert peoples ideal shelters.

The frameworks of Columbia Plateau pithouses (below) seem to have been built above different types of excavations. Some of these were as much as five feet deep and featured an earthen shelf running around the perimeter; others were not so deep and the shelf was omitted. In most, walls were vertical, but some were no more than shallow saucers with sloping walls. The shape invariably was round or oval.

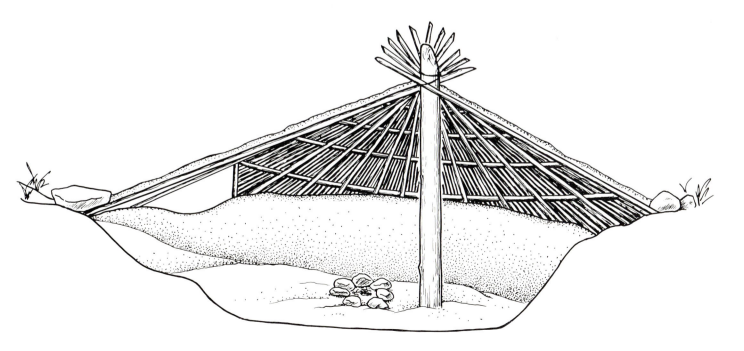

Pole length determined the maximum size of the houses, with the exact floor diameter depending on how the poles were set. Spreading them increased diameter, but at the cost of height. This loss was remedied by digging the pit deeper, which restored height even close against the walls. Families on foot were limited to the size of poles most immediately available and to the lightest serviceable covering, the mats. Size and weight became less crucial after the acquisition of horses. In Washington this means about 1730 when the descendants of mounts originally brought by Spanish conquistadors spread this far north. Houses as much as thirty to forty feet across then became common, for horse travel eliminated the need to use whatever size poles were close at hand. Hide-covered teepees, an idea borrowed from Plains Indians, also came into widespread use; so did elongated A-frame mat houses, which amounted to stretched-out versions of circular mat-covered pithouses.

This aspect of mobility is fundamental to understanding the past. Man on foot knew few travel restrictions. He wasn't limited to waterways or to the routes offered by valleys or beaches. On the other hand, travel often was slow and difficult, and he couldn't carry much with him. Material possessions were few. Settled life in villages favored the acquisition of belongings. In a similar way, the fashioning of watercraft and the use of horses facilitated the transport of goods. For millennia Plateau life revolved around travel between winter villages and root-digging and berry-picking camps, hunting grounds, and fishing stations. This mobility dictated the types of containers that were used. They were baskets and skin parfleches, practical to take along on seasonal rounds. Agricultural peoples developed pottery for containers and cooking. Mobile peoples—which includes all of those in Washington—didn't make pottery. It is too heavy to carry and too easily broken.

Current excavation along the fifty miles of the Columbia River between Chief Joseph and Grand Coulee dams promises to yield additional insight into patterns of this seasonal movement. Small pithouse villages (dating from 2,700 B.P. into the historic period) seem associated with nearby fishing camps, hunting camps, pictographs, and cairns generally believed to mark ritual quests for guardian spirits. Artifacts so far include microblades from six-thousand-year-old sites, projectile points, milling stones, mauls, antler wedges, stone and bone beads, needles and awls. More than 250 sites have been located, 50 of them sufficiently intact to warrant testing and excavating by the University of Washington Office of Public Archaeology. Work will continue until 1981, by which time the level of the reservoir will have been raised ten feet to supply water for additional power generation. Colville Indian tribal members are working with the archaeologists in this recovery of their ancestral past, and artifacts and data are to be held in trust by the United States Army Corps of Engineers until the Colvilles have their own means of storage and/or display.

Salmon vertebrae from the Miller Site (top); bones from butchered elk and bison, some cracked open to extract marrow (bottom).

The largest remaining pithouse village known on the Plateau is the Miller Site on Strawberry Island, close to the confluence of the Snake River with the Columbia. Occupation goes back at least one thousand years, resulting in a complex archaeological puzzle: in the process of reexcavating houses through the centuries villagers disrupted layers and turned time contexts upside down. More than one hundred pits are present. Most probably were houses, a few may have been for sweat houses, and several must represent pits and earth ovens.

Elsewhere along the river, village sites have been flooded by reservoirs, and even at Strawberry Island the opportunity for investigation is fragile. Water backed by McNary Dam floods the lower rim of the island, and barge traffic sends waves cutting into the shore, washing away unstable sand and silt deposits. Investigation here by Washington State University archaeologist Greg Cleveland in 1976 and 1977 will continue for several more summers under the direction of Randall Schalk. So far there is evidence of elk and bison hunting and of fishing, and a "workshop" with about four hundred hammerstones and anvils has been found. Schalk hopes to trace patterns of usage within the village. For instance, small pits with about twenty square feet of floor space are clustered across the island from those with two hundred to six hundred square feet of space. Perhaps the small ones were for storage; the large ones, dwellings. Interestingly, among the likely dwellings are two pits with floors of more than twelve hundred square feet. These have no hearths. That fact, together with their large size, suggests they may have been communal structures of some sort.

Sediments removed from site excavations were shaken through quarter-inch screens to recover small artifacts and bone fragments that otherwise might have been overlooked.

At Alpowa the study of pithouses has revealed remarkable detail of indoor living arrangements. Twelve houses sampled there during three field seasons, 1970–72, range in age from the earliest known on the Plateau—about five thousand years old—to slightly over one thousand years old. David Brauner, at the time a Washington State University doctoral candidate working under Frank Leonhardy, and now at Oregon State University, directed excavation. One house had been an oval about thirty feet long. No post holes indicated the location or nature of the superstructure that had covered its floor, which was dug only about a foot into the ground. Probably this was a mat house, and when people moved they dismantled it and took with them what they could, leaving behind heavy objects and mislaid objects. Brauner found twenty-three projectile points, six knives, two drills, one graver, seven scrapers, a shaft abrader, choppers, an antler wedge, the base of a mortar that must once have been fitted with a basketry hopper, three anvil stones, a bone pendant, shell and soapstone beads, and a paint palette. Such remnants tell a good deal about the house.

The projectile points lay distributed as though they belonged to two hunters who shared the house—the small ones on one side of the hearth, large ones on the other. Or perhaps one set was for an atlatl-dart system, the other for a bow and arrows. Cryptocrystalline blanks to be flaked into points also were present. The beads and pendant were close to the mortar base and anvils, the food processing centers where women must have spent a great deal of time. Around one of the anvils were cobbles apparently intended as hammerstones, and with them was a scattering of shattered bone. Along one wall a pile of river cobbles, perhaps used as net sinkers, suggested fishing.

Another house had twelve distinct activity centers: three for food preparation, one for working hides, one for making basketry and cordage, one for bone working, two for lithic manufacturing and repair, and four for general manufacturing. Scrapers suggested the hide working; awls the basketry and cordage; various types of debris the other activities.

In a third house details of food preparation areas were particularly clear. There were two, situated one on each side of an entry ramp (the first such ramp known for Plateau houses). The pattern of debris around the anvil stones indicated that the women using them must have sat facing the ramp where they had light from the doorway for their work, as well as from the fire and the smokehole. This position was out of the main traffic flow of the house, yet the anvils were convenient to where meat was brought in. Mortars sat close to the hearth in this house. Beside them were rocks cracked by heat, probably used for cooking in baskets. The method was to first heat the rocks in a fire, then drop them into baskets of water.

Handles for digging sticks (opposite, above) usually were made of deer or elk antler, often elaborately incised. At least in historic times a young girl might be given such a handle, which she then would keep for life. Petroglyphs (left and opposite) are designs pecked into rock cliffs, their significance long-since lost. Blasting for railroads and highways has destroyed some; many have been inundated by reservoirs along the Columbia and Snake rivers.

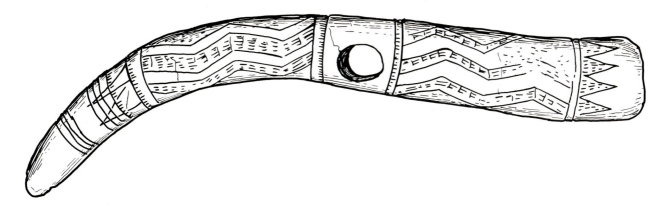

Such details whisper of everyday life: the comings and goings of hunters and fishermen and root diggers, adults and children. Generation followed generation at Alpowa and over the Plateau as a whole. The pattern of life varied geographically but basically was one of living together at the winter village, drawing on stores of dried fish and roots, then scattering to begin a series of gathering, hunting, and fishing rounds. Several families roamed together on these excursions, moving camp as resources dictated. Mats taken from winter pithouses were used as teepee covers or as mere circular windbreaks. Generally poles were cut anew at each camping place. New anvil stones for use in cracking open bones to extract marrow were easily found; and it took only minutes to knock a few flakes from the edges of cobbles for a new set of hammerstones. Mortars for grinding and pounding plant foods also were easily replaced. A single flat stone provided the base, and the basketry hopper that encircled it was lightweight and easy to pack along.

Little archaeological evidence of these food-gathering rounds can be expected. The camps were transient, and the process of harvesting vegetation leaves little trace beyond that soon lost to decay. Ethnographic evidence, however, gives insight into what the seasonal rounds must have been. Also, Indian families today still follow many of the old practices, and archaeologists themselves are digging roots and gathering materials in order to understand as fully as possible what kinds of evidence may be expected to remain.

Roots are ready to dig at low elevations by early April and at successively higher elevations as the season progresses. The necessary tools were nothing more than sharpened sticks, for convenience usually fitted with wooden or antler handles. Experienced diggers, women only, probably covered about a half an acre per day. In that time they could harvest as much as a bushel of roots—camas, onion, bitterroot, biscuitroot, and others. These were carried to camp for sorting in bags woven of willow bark or Indian hemp. Any roots damaged in digging were set aside for eating fresh. The others, depending on their species, were baked in shallow pits filled with heated stones and covered over, or they were pulverized and patted into cakes to be spread onto mats and dried in the sun. Some roots were strung and dried whole.

*Roots such as camas still are dug by Indian peo-
ple—and by archaeologists. Yakimas hold
traditional root ceremonies in mid–April on the
sites of former winter villages.*

After the root season came the berry season—currants and
chokecherries on wooded hillsides, huckleberries on the slopes
of mountain foothills and in alpine meadows. While women
gathered and processed such resources, men hunted antelope,
deer, and elk. Both meat and hides are at their best during summer rather than in autumn during rut when most hunting is
done today. Bighorn sheep and mountain goats were hunted for
horn to use in making spoons and bowls, as well as for meat;
and the goats also provided hair, which was prized for spinning
into yarn. As summer merged into fall, salmon began to arrive
even in the upper reaches of the Snake and Columbia river sys-
tems, and families moved to fish camps. Then came winter and a
return to the villages.

The moves were regular, coming in the same sequence, at the
same times of year, and usually involving the same sites. Life
was patterned, rhythmical. It also was egalitarian and peace-
able. Resources were equally available to all. Little property
management was entailed in their utilization; chieftainships,
courts, and councils weren't needed. Individuals were all fairly
equal. Fish camps, particularly, became centers of trade and social exchange, open to all. Certain groups held proprietary rights
to fishing stations, but these never were exclusive. Anyone could
participate simply by asking. At least by a thousand years ago,
and perhaps also long before, Kettle Falls had become a major
trade center. Similarly, by historic times and probably earlier,
Wakemap on the lower Columbia was an even greater focal
point. Its geographic position brought the ideas, techniques, and
commodities of people from the interior into contact with those
from the coast. Elsewhere, mountains separated east from west,
not wholly but substantially. The Columbia belonged to both.

What ultimately might have happened within Plateau culture
can never be known. Its development came from within for more
than ten thousand years; then the whole lifeway was truncated
by the arrival of whites. Epidemics killed more than half of the
population. Circumstances changed so totally that survivors
couldn't pick up many threads from their past. They were forced
to weave a whole new fabric of life, part of its strands belonging
to their heritage, most growing out of alien products and con-
cepts. The long continuity had been broken.

Yakima women today pick huckleberries on the slopes of Mount Adams (top). In the old days alpine camps afforded a chance to hunt mountain goats (above, right) for their horn and fleece. The woolly hair was spun into yarn using spindles with whorls to hold the accumulating yarn (above, left).

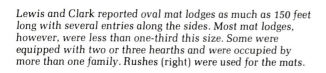

Lewis and Clark reported oval mat lodges as much as 150 feet long with several entries along the sides. Most mat lodges, however, were less than one-third this size. Some were equipped with two or three hearths and were occupied by more than one family. Rushes (right) were used for the mats.

Teepees seem to have come to the Plateau as contact with Plains Indians increased following acquisition of the horse. At first, mat coverings still predominated, slowly giving way to hide and canvas.

The triangular shape of the axe blade helped hold the head tight as it was forced into the handle through use. Pressure alone held it in place; no notching was necessary. Archaeologist Jeff Flenniken tested a replicated axe (above) by chopping through a piece of willow. Ponderosa pine (right) and abundant mule deer (opposite, bottom) are typical of higher elevations on the Columbia Plateau.

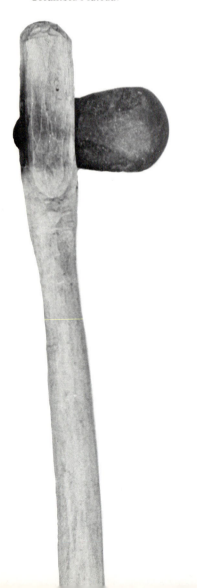

Flenniken used sinew softened in his mouth to attach feathers to an arrow he was making (left). Sinew is sticky enough to hold without knotting or gluing if it is wrapped into place while wet. With grooved sandstone abraders (above) Flenniken rounded and smoothed the shaft of the arrow. Willow was favored for shafts because it is flexible enough to straighten readily.

The Coast

Traveling along the north shore of the Columbia River near The Dalles in 1805, men on the Lewis and Clark Expedition noted the first wooden houses they had seen since leaving Illinois—a village of twenty houses "scattered promiscuously" near an earthen mound thirty feet high with "some remains of houses" apparent within. This was the village of Wakemap, one of several in the vicinity situated to take advantage of fishing where river constrictions concentrated the salmon runs. The village marked the farthest inland point known for a house style belonging to the coast, an intriguing reflection of the lower Columbia's position as mingling ground for Plateau and Northwest Coast cultures. Wakemap itself dates back at least two thousand years; directly across the river from it is The Dalles' Five Mile Rapids site with the valuable eleven-thousand-year sequence.

Today the conspicuous features of the Wakemap area are a railroad, the slack water of a manmade lake, and a state park. Go farther downriver and the large village site of Neechakeoo mentioned by Lewis and Clark is covered by runways of the Portland airport; another village—its name unknown—lies beneath the municipal garbage dump. On Sauvies Island near Portland workmen excavating a basement on top of a mound dug up quantities of bone, antler, and stone artifacts, including delicately carved figures. While putting in a septic tank below the mound, they cross-sectioned the stratified deposits of six or seven hundred years of human habitation. Near Vancouver, on the Washington side of the river, a proposed highway route prompted investigation of a site so rich archaeologically that two summers of work yielded ten thousand artifacts—and relocation of the intended highway.

The fate of lower Columbia prehistory has been to remain largely unknown, much of its record lost to twentieth-century construction and to relic hunters collecting mere objects. Even more has been lost to the erosion of river banks. Nonetheless, by investigating remaining sites, archaeologists hope fairly soon to work out reasonable detail. Major excavation currently is underway below Bonneville Dam with opportunity for study of a village site several hundred years old and recovery of abundant artifacts. So far, nearly one thousand net weights and canoe anchor stones have been found. There also have been examples of the basalt effigies, pestles, and bowls for which the lower Columbia is noted. They represent a distinctive art style unfortunately heretofore known more from private collections than from artifacts studied in context. Such objects are rare elsewhere in Washington, although some stone sculpture has come from the lower Skagit River and is fairly common along the lower Fraser River in British Columbia. What the cultural implications of this distribution may be aren't yet understood.

"Shoto clay"—so-called for a historic-period Lower Columbia village where examples have been found—includes human faces (opposite) and enigmatic tablets (above, top). Such pieces, along with stone bowls, pestles, and figurines (above, bottom), come mostly from the Lower Columbia. Some of the clay is partly fired, perhaps fortuitously during cremation. The age of such pieces is unknown. (Clay tablets and smaller face shown here actual size; larger face, size unrecorded; owl one-sixth actual size.)

In some ways archaeological field work in western Washington is more difficult than it is east of the Cascades. Rank vegetation conceals sites and complicates locating those that aren't uncovered by chance during construction work or by erosion. Along the coast, tidal action has destroyed scores of sites. Others have been flooded by salt water, or lifted above today's beach, as sea level has changed; some have become inland sites due to the formation of deltas. Dynamism enhances coastal appeal—and also complicates the work of archaeologists.

Perhaps partly because of this geologic instability, early evidence of man in western Washington has come from sites inland from today's coast, or on terraces above present sea level. This may indicate that the first bands of people were more skilled at using land and river resources than those of the salt water and beach; or the sites may represent the inland hunting and gathering rounds of people who at other times used coastal resources. Since much of the previous coast now lies underwater, most of early man's beach campsites aren't likely to be found.

Until discovery of the Sequim mastodon with its date of at least 12,000 B.P., "early" sites west of the Cascades were considered those from about 9,000 to 6,000 B.P. These are termed "Olcott sites" for the owners of property on the Stillaguamish River near Arlington, where archaeologists first recovered a sizeable assemblage of the artifacts. About five hundred pounds of basalt flakes, spalls, and cores, together with finished choppers, a few scrapers and knife blades, and scores of projectile points came from a terrace there well above the present river, although at the time of occupancy probably fairly close to it. Most lay in a field, seemingly plowed to the surface. In shape and workmanship these points match willow leaf points found east of the Cascades.

Similar artifacts came from a site near Quilcene, at the head of Hood Canal, in 1971. What now is an upland above Quilcene Bay seems to have formed as a delta feeding first into ice-age Lake Russell and later into salt water which lapped the land 100 to 125 feet above the surface of the present-day bay. Artifacts here, excavated under the direction of Washington State Highways archaeologist David Munsell, included twenty fragments and three complete willow leaf points of basalt, twenty chopper-like cobbles with flakes removed, three cobbles with an edge sharpened by grinding, ninety-nine scrapers of eight distinct types, ten gravers and burins (pointed tools seemingly for drilling or incising), two sandstone milling stones, and five split sandstone cobbles with longitudinal grooves that must have been for smoothing wooden or bone shafts.

Analyzing the artifacts, which at Quilcene were found *in situ*, Munsell could venture a few tentative conclusions. Chips of stone lying in elliptical patterns seemed to indicate individual toolmaking areas. The abundance of scrapers suggested that people had been dressing hides. The groove of an abrader was flared at the ends, apparently the result of tapering and sharpening bone awls or needles. Several projectile points and burins stood point down in the sandy soil, and milling stones and sharpened cobbles were on edge. Seemingly this position was deliberate, as though to prevent loss.

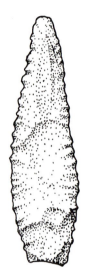

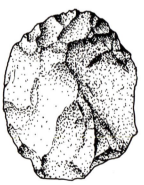

Willow-leaf point and scraper of basalt, Quilcene.

Probably the Quilcene people—and those of all Olcott sites—were hunters; what else they may have been can't well be known since nothing but stone remains. The tools are widespread. Show a map to someone who has specialized in Olcott material, such as Munsell, and he can pinpoint sites with the telltale willow leaf points and cobble choppers in the San Juan Islands, around Bellingham, Ferndale, Arlington, Anacortes, Kent, Mossyrock, Chehalis, Montesano, Kelso, Monroe, Taholah, and a dozen other locations. At most of these, determining age is difficult because the sites lack organic material suitable for radiocarbon dating. The time span of 9,000 to 6,000 B.P., which is considered likely for Olcott artifacts, is based on their position within geologic sequences and their similarity with eastern Washington counterparts at sites dated by carbon-14.

Five early sites in western Washington that have been radiocarbon dated are located within a few miles of each other on the Enumclaw Plateau. Occupation goes back to 6,000 B.P. in an area where geologic dating of a dramatic sort also is present, in the form of the Osceola mudflow. Originating near the summit of Mount Rainier about five thousand years ago, this cementlike flow veneered an area of sixty-five square miles, filling valleys and overtopping low hills. Boulders as much as three feet in diameter were borne along by a matrix of clay, their size suggesting a velocity of at least fifty miles per hour. While probing into the mudflow deposits in 1973, students working with Gerald Hedlund of Green River Community College found a rounded cobble with one edge sharpened by grinding. Within the next four years from beneath the mudflow they found more than three hundred additional artifacts—points, scrapers, gravers, drills, and cobble tools. They also located hearths and the charcoal that was used in dating. Seemingly the pre-mudflow people had been camping along the shore of a lake or marsh. If any were present at the time of the catastrophe, they must have been killed or isolated on high ground surrounded by a sea of sterile mud.

People could have moved back within two or three decades following the devastation, judging from the rapid recovery of plants and animals following a similar but less extensive mudflow in 1947 at Kautz Creek, on the south side of Mount Rainier. Clearly, people did return, for stone artifacts were found above the mudflow. Most of these are made from chalcedony, jasper, or chert, whereas those below the mudflow are of basalt or andesite. This seems to indicate a cultural difference between the people present before the mudflow and those who returned afterward, but details have not been worked out. Hedlund found pithouses above the mudflow but no traces of cedar plank houses. Subsistence seemingly followed the widespread hunting and gathering pattern familiar east of the Cascades and at western Olcott sites.

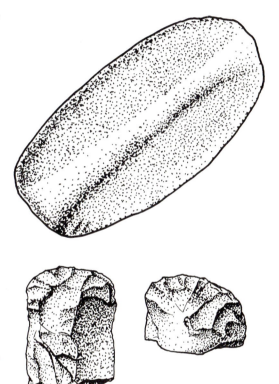

Abrader and scrapers, Quilcene. The abrader seems to have been used for grinding points on awls or needles.

83

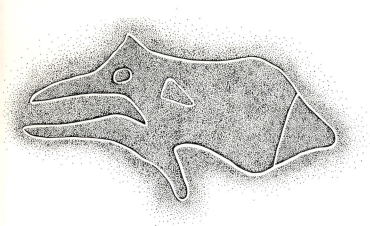

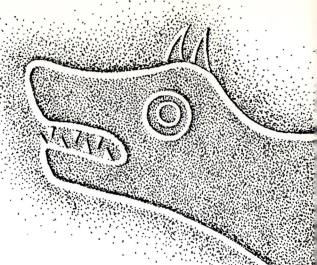

This broad dependence characterized the coast as well as the uplands. In fact man at first seems to have made little use of coastal resources even while at the shore, although evidence is difficult to assess. Boats of some sort were available quite early, at least on the northern coast, for a large village site at Anangula in the eastern Aleutian Islands dates from 8,000 B.P., and human habitation began in the Queen Charlotte Islands of British Columbia at about the same time. Both of these island locations necessitated some means of crossing open water. An even earlier indication of watercraft comes from the Prince Rupert region. At Namu archaeologists working in deposits that date to 9,000 B.P. found the remains of sea otters, sea lions, and porpoises—mammals that can be taken only at sea. Their presence indicates seamanship as well as the existence of boats.

Whether people on the Washington coast had watercraft at that time isn't known. No sites of comparable age have been found; indeed those that may once have been there probably now lie underwater. Curtis Larsen, working as a graduate student under Dr. Garland Grabert at Western Washington University, made a study of where man could have lived at Birch Bay through the last twelve millennia. Data included bathymetric measurement and calculation of isostatic and eustatic effects on sea level. From them Larsen concluded that cobble tools found on terraces above today's sea level may date from as early as ten thousand years ago but that any occupation sites belonging to the next five-thousand-year period now are underwater. Interestingly, this time span correlates to a recognized hiatus in archaeological data: coast sites of that age simply are not known in Washington presumably owing to the raised ocean level caused by ice melt at the close of the Pleistocene.

Only a few sites dating from the period immediately following this knowledge gap are known. At Birch Bay there are two dating from four to five thousand years ago—about the time that sea level stabilized at its present position—but neither indicates much about the people camped there. Artifacts include cobble and flake tools, basalt projectile points, a burin, and small stones that may have been used with slings for hunting waterfowl or tied into woven bags for use as net sinkers. On San Juan Island, sites nearly three thousand years old suggest that people initially relied mostly on deer and other land resources even though living on the island. They only slowly increased their use of fish and shellfish. Perhaps they moved from the mainland because of population pressure or to escape harassment rather than specifically for the rich saltwater resources of San Juan.

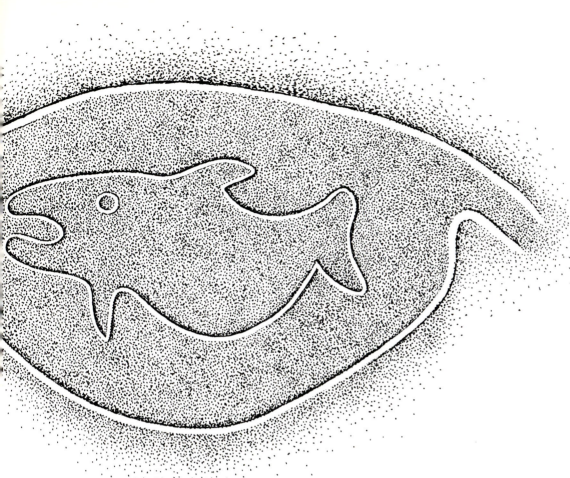

At the Glenrose Cannery site on the Fraser River delta just
north of the Washington border, extensive deposits span almost
continuously from 8,000 to 2,000 B.P. Excavation there from
1969 to 1973—and analysis of data during the next two years—
clearly indicate a gradual increase in use of the foreshore. Few
shellfish remains are present in the oldest deposits, but at about
four thousand years ago they become abundant. In fact calculation of the amount of meat represented by the shell suggests that
mussels and clams were equal in importance to the meat of deer,
elk, and seal from 4,000 to 3,000 B.P.

Seasonal growth rings on the shells, something like those familiar in tree trunks, show that people at Glenrose at first collected mollusks in spring and summer, then finally only in
winter. This tendency toward winter use points to what probably was man's main advantage in living at the coast. Shore and
ocean resources are little affected by weather and season, which
drastically alter terrestial resources. Shellfish offered a dependable year-round answer to hunger (except for times of red tide);
bottomfish could be taken even when salmon weren't available;
game and plant foods remained as accessible as at inland locations. Storms might complicate winter travel at times, but calm
seas and moderate temperatures are characteristic of
Washington coastal winters.

*Petroglyphs along the northern Washington
coast testify to the importance of maritime resources. Wedding Rock figure (opposite); Ar-
chawat figure (above).*

Details of maritime development can't be traced from the few sites known so far, which makes protection and scientific investigation of what there are all the more important. Certainly by its culmination, and probably long before, man's adaptation to shore and water had become infinitely varied and superbly tuned. So efficient, for example, were techniques of fishing that Indian people had no reason to revamp methods or the basic designs of gear even after the arrival of Europeans and Americans. Only materials changed. Metal fishhooks were simply substituted for bone; hemp rope, for lines of kelp and twisted cedar boughs; and linen thread, for the nettle fiber and willow bark of earlier nets. Indian fishermen still aligned stones in great vees and half-circles where fish would swim over the tops on a high tide and be trapped by the low tide. Where migrating salmon crossed kelp reefs, Indians cut pathways leading to where harpooners waited in canoes. Sometimes they lined the sea bottom beneath these paths with light-colored rocks to make the fish show up better. Men trolled, used gill nets, trawl nets, dip nets, seines, harpoons, and leisters. Along the Strait of Juan de Fuca and in northern Puget Sound, reef netting was of paramount importance, involving a whole complex of technical, ritual, and social activities.

The reef net was as much as forty feet long by thirty feet wide, dyed dark to reduce visibility. Weights held down its leading edge, which faced into the current; the aft edge was drawn taut near the surface between two canoes anchored parallel to each other and manned with crews of six to twelve men. A web of floating lines formed an inclined trough leading from the sea bottom. Sometimes bunches of rye grass tied at intervals across the floor lines of the trough enhanced the illusion of sea bottom and encouraged the sockeye to swim into the net. A captain in the canoe farthest offshore directed the crew to pull the net when he saw fish swim over its leading edge. The two canoes then swung together and the crews hauled the net into the inshore canoe, spilling the fish into the offshore one. Visibility into the water was essential, which limited the operation to fine days and calm seas. At the height of runs several thousand fish could be taken this way in a single day.

At the Port of Tacoma, archaeologists excavated a fish weir estimated to be 400 to 1,000 years old.

Such detail comes from early-day journals and ethnographic reports rather than from the archaeological record, where sequences usually are difficult to correlate to one another and perishable materials such as wood, hide, and fiber generally are missing altogether. Few sites yield unique information or showy artifacts, though all contribute to the patient detective work of piecing together the mosaic of human life. Often a site's chief public interest rests in its location. For instance, at Wapato Creek, flowing into the Port of Tacoma, David Munsell in 1970 excavated the remains of a fish weir thought to be from four hundred to one thousand years old. It was chanced upon by a contractor dredging for a new loading facility. Upright stakes supported a wattle of Douglas-fir branches twined with red cedar boughs, and a net of split cedar root and twisted cedar bark still clung to part of it.

A different glimpse of prehistory was discovered at the Port of Seattle during the construction of a new loading facility on the Duwamish waterway in 1976. This site, occupied from about 1,300 to 200 B.P., had a fairly high concentration of tools and probable evidence of a cedar plank house—a chance for the Duwamish Indian people to recover their past and, to date, the earliest chapter in the saga of Seattle's habitation available for archaeological investigation. Sarah Campbell, University of Washington graduate student directing excavations at this site, hopes to document changes in the estuary through time as well as the pattern of human life there: shells within the midden gradually shift from salt-tolerant species to those found in fresh water. The environment changed, and the archaeological deposits may explain why.

Two sites excavated during the 1970s by Astrida Onat, archaeologist at Seattle Community College, offer insight into the nature of permanent settlements along Puget Sound shores. These are Indian Island, southeast of Port Townsend, and Swikwikwab, on the Skagit delta, both radiocarbon dated at somewhat older than 1,000 B.P.

The Indian Island site is situated on a sandspit that has been stable for the last ten centuries, whereas other spits in the region are eroding, washing archaeological sites into the water. Evidence as to whether occupation of the spit was seasonal or year-round at first seemed contradictory. Artifacts suggested that people were coming seasonally to catch bottomfish and herring, and there were no indications of other sorts of activities such as would be expected if occupation were permanent. On the other hand, post holes and a carefully tended, packed earth floor suggested a much more substantial dwelling than would be likely at a temporary camp. At times the house must have been occupied year-round. Probably it belonged to one of the adjacent villages, which seemed distant as viewed from the land but were actually close-by for people with canoes. Water was a uniting factor. A lone house wasn't cut off, it simply stood at village outskirts—a forerunner of suburbs.

Five antler figures virtually identical except for size have been found at widespread locations along the Northwest Coast. This one, shown one and a half times actual size, was found at Swikwikwab on the Skagit delta. Others—some only fragmentary—have come from Conway, Sucia Island, the Gulf Islands, and Bella Coola, British Columbia.

Fossil cockle and iron-bladed chisel, Minard site. The fossil must represent a curiosity picked up along the beach long ago.

A similar situation prevailed on the Skagit delta where four individual sites are clustered on what once was an island that now lies well inland, swallowed by the delta's expansion. Each site is separate from the others and each indicated a different kind of usage as people exploited specific environmental situations; yet the four were within easy walking distance of each other. Should they be viewed as separate habitations or as parts of a whole? One site had served as a housing area. A former swamp nearby held waterlogged fragments of large carrying baskets and stakes still upright as though for a fish weir or as supports for a set net. Deer, elk, and seal bones were concentrated on a hillside; and on the former tideflat below were bird and fish bones. Several thousand salmon vertebrae came from a single five-inch layer of a six-foot excavation square, perhaps indication of a huge feast or an enormous fish run, or both. Bird bone, too, was uncommonly abundant—not surprising since the area is on the flyway of migratory waterfowl. Considered separately, each site would indicate a different subsistence base for its occupants. Yet probably all four represent a single settlement.

Overall, life at the edge of the sea followed much the same pattern all along the Northwest coast. Perhaps the major difference lies in the extensive hunting of sea mammals by people on the outer coast, but not by those living on Puget Sound or along the Strait of Juan de Fuca—or even by all peoples on the Pacific coast. Consider, for example, the Martin, Minard, and Ozette sites. All date to something earlier than 1,000 B.P. with the Martin site nearly two thousand years old and the Ozette site probably older still.

Martin and Minard, located respectively on the Long Beach peninsula at Willapa Bay and near Ocean Shores at Grays Harbor, belong to a region of sheltered bays and long straight sand beaches washed by a rolling surf. Canoe travel on the bays and up the rivers emptying into them was easy, and at Martin the parallel ridges of the Long Beach peninsula bordered stringlike lakes that permitted additional miles of water travel. Ocean launchings and landings, on the other hand, were difficult because of the surf.

Ozette's setting contrasts with this. Situated about fifteen miles south of Cape Flattery, its beach is a crescent protected by points of land and faced offshore by a reef and small islands. Ocean canoeing was readily feasible, and the reef offered rich resources. Migrating fur seals, furthermore, follow the one-hundred-fathom contour of the continental shelf, which at Ozette is thirty miles offshore. At the southern sites the one-hundred-fathom line lies three times farther seaward.

The Martin and Minard sites face the quiet water of the bays and, though the ocean shore is close-by, people barely used its resources. Faunal remains show deer, elk, hare, and harbor seal as of primary importance, and abundant stone projectile points bear out the emphasis on land resources. Digging stick handles suggest a considerable use of roots, although probably the same sticks also were used to dig clams. Oysters, cockles, razor clams, and horse clams were the species most common at the Martin site, compared with bent-nose clams, cockles, bay mussels, and razor clams at the Minard site. Quantities of salmon bones indicate the basic importance of fish at both sites. At Minard they apparently were taken mostly with small toggling harpoons and probably also nets, whereas at Martin no harpoons were found, suggestion of a basic reliance on nets (which left no direct evidence).

Washington State University graduate student Tom Roll in 1974 compared these data with the Ozette situation and found a decided north–south difference. Salmon bones are relatively few at Ozette, but halibut and ling cod are well represented. Shellfish are primarily California and blue mussel, periwinkle, littleneck clam, and sea urchin. Mammal remains are mostly fur seal, whale, porpoise, dolphin, and sea lion. Elk and deer bones also are present but are inconsequential compared with the others. Only one or two stone projectile points have been found, but other types may have been used. For instance, barbed bone points found at the site would cause a mortal wound even when delivered by the relatively small bows known to be typical at Ozette.

All three sites are on the ocean coast—two days apart by canoe given favorable conditions—yet the specializations of their people differed substantially. At Martin and Minard, spawning salmon thronged the labyrinthine waterways and if one run was poor others probably were normal. If harbor seals were not hauled out on islands within the bays, convenient to hunt, additional deer and elk were readily available in the forest. Most sea mammals passed by too far offshore to be worth hunting. At Ozette both opportunity and cultural preferences for food produced a very different pattern. Here men fished at sea and hunted whales and fur seals. If these migrants failed to arrive in usual numbers people must have been inconvenienced.

Characteristically the resource base of all Northwest coast villages was so rich that if disaster struck one element within it others usually sufficed. Stored foods helped, so did the ready availability of shellfish. Furthermore the potlatch system of huge giveaways efficiently evened out shortages that might otherwise have been troublesome. This was an important means of "coping with abundance" as Wayne Suttles, anthropologist at Portland State University, expresses it.

Here were a people without agricultural crops or herds, yet with an elaborate culture. How early it became thus nobody can say, but at least by 1,000 B.P. people were living in villages with populations of several hundred, their houses built of planks split from cedar. Probably adults quite routinely were speaking two or three languages, as was true in historic times and to some extent is still true among Indian elders. Long-distance canoe travel facilitated both seasonal rounds and a social network that reached far beyond the immediate village. Specialists took charge of the various types of hunting and fishing, the manufacture of tools and implements, and curing. Elaborate ceremonies went on for days at a time, particularly in winter, much of their effect dependent on carvings now recognized as one of the world's great art styles. Personal inheritance and economic success provided a rigid ranking system that included slave and nonslave, and within the nonslave division ranged from commoner through noble.

Antler carving, Minard site; actual height: 3½". From the historic period, the figure appears dressed in a regimental greatcoat and is holding the barrel of a flintlock rifle or musket, the butt resting on the ground. To this Euro–American depiction is added the traditional Northwest Coast dot-and-circle motif.

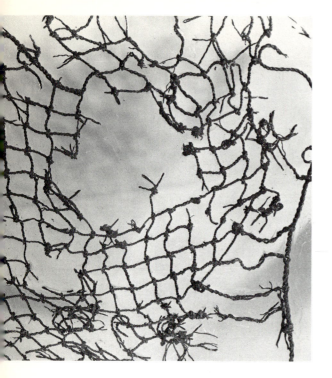

With their rich habitat of the saltwater shore, coast people still followed the ages-old subsistence pattern of harvesting seasonal abundance. They traveled and camped to make the rounds of land and waters. Since each category within the overall largesse was available only temporarily, maximizing potential benefit required measures beyond simply getting food and storing it. Also needed was a system of exchange. On occasion even small streams would yield thousands of salmon; hundreds of waterfowl could be taken at a marsh during migration; a single sturgeon might weigh nearly a ton and a whale somewhere around thirty tons. But all of this came "on occasion"—certain things, at certain times, in certain places, and always with the possibility of failure. Stormy seas might make halibut fishing impossible. Unexpected rains could spoil the drying salmon. The berry crop might prove poor several years in succession. These times of least supply, not the favorable ones, were what determined the level at which population could be maintained.

In Suttles' opinion it was the Northwest Coast prestige system that provided a way of handling occasional scarcity. Simple awareness of possible, but unlikely, hard times could give little incentive for storing winter food each year; but preparing for a known season of ceremony would achieve the same result, especially when that ceremony entailed feasting and validating wealth by giving it away to assembled guests. This was the potlatch: a proclamation of status built on giving people from the home village and from villages far distant immense quantities of material goods—food, artwork, slaves—and also on performing songs and dances for one another. The gifts dealt with surplus in a way that brought honor far beyond that of selling or trading, yet in economic terms they amounted to a redistribution of food and goods. The songs and dances, elaborately costumed and staged, laid claim to prestige. The prestige lent momentum to the whole system.

Within that framework, even economic pursuits often were geared toward achieving status more than toward holding off hunger. Whaling furnishes an illustration. Along the southern coast of Vancouver Island and the northwestern coast of the Olympic Peninsula men, eight in a canoe, paddled to sea to hunt whales. Elaborate ritual attended this pursuit, its correctness to the last detail as important a preparation as the careful maintenance of the canoe and whaling gear itself. Only men from wealthy families could afford to venture after whales, and the right was hereditary rather than available to all. A single whale successfully towed to the home village provided vast amounts of oil, bone, and meat—and prestige. No families received more deference than that accorded whalers' families, a feeling still faintly echoed along the Olympic coast as Makah and Quileute people speak of relatives who hunted whales.

Probably both the prestige and the practice of whaling reach into the past at least two thousand years. The Ozette site gives a chance to study the matter in detail. The village there was located at the westernmost point of the Washington coast, miles closer than any other village to the migration routes of whales—grays, humpbacks, sperm whales, right whales, and others. This was a great enough advantage that Ozette became one of the major whaling villages south of Alaska.

Fish net and basket, each nearly 500 years old, from buried house at Ozette (left). Flat bag woven of cedarbark, also from Ozette (opposite). Such bags were traditional among Makah whalers. A pair was found in House One, each holding harpoon heads sheathed in folded cedarbark.

Deep midden there attracted the attention of Dr. Richard Daugherty while still a graduate student, and nearly twenty years later he had students dig a trench to cross-section the deposits. It cut for two hundred feet from today's high-tide line up through four previous beaches rising as terraces behind it. Radiocarbon dating gave an age of 1,600 years for part of the trench, and geologist Roald Fryxell estimated that strata not sampled for carbon must be two or three times older than that.

For all that time the midden lay without apparent break in continuity. Carl Gustafson analyzed a sample from 80,000 animal bones found in the trench and reported no species change from layer to layer. Whalebones were there from the first, massive protrusions jutting out of trench walls; also a certain type of barnacle that lives only on the skin of whales suggested that some of the final butchering may have taken place within the village itself rather than on the beach. A host of artifacts ranged from harpoons and knives to spindle whorls and awls, whistles, gambling pieces, and combs. Particular concentrations of objects often correlated with the position of hearths or of post molds where upright supports once had been, indications of ancient house floors.

The following summer—1967—archaeology students again converged on the site, this time to investigate a slope were photographs from the 1890s showed several houses to have stood. Ozette was occupied until the 1920s when families reluctantly moved to Neah Bay so their children could be in school. People still returned in summer to fish and hunt, however.

Excavation of the historic houses went routinely, with recovery of items such as broken china and glass bottles, shoe-button hooks and coins along with stone and bone tools, bits of clamshell and whale bones. Then unexpected discoveries began. At the edge of the beach a wet area yielded perfectly preserved rope twisted from cedar boughs and fragments of cedar-bark mats and baskets. Up the slope, a test pit nine feet deep reached a muddy zone and revealed a cedar plank with pieces of baskets and additional planks beneath it. This tied with Makah legends of a landslide sweeping into the Ozette village, burying houses. Fryxell had mapped several slide deposits along the slope; furthermore, the overburden covering the planks and baskets in the test pit was clay, a likely mudflow material.

Additional investigation wasn't immediately possible because the summer season was at an end, funds had run out, and work at Marmes Rockshelter was reaching a critical stage, the human skeletal material newly discovered and little time remaining until reservoir waters would flood the site. Daugherty ordered the pit closed. Buried houses would be too valuable to excavate on anything less than a full-scale basis.

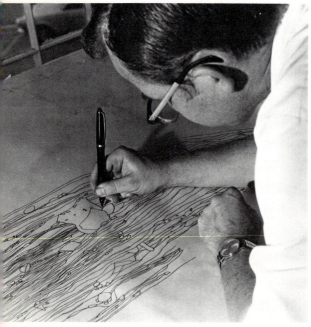

In 1966, a 200-foot trench was dug at Ozette (above) to cross-section the midden deposits of a series of terraces rising above today's beach, the uppermost one the oldest. A stratigraphic drawing (left) recorded the layers exposed in the trench walls along with rocks, whale bones, artifacts, and fire hearths and postholes left by the ancient houses.

Three years later that kind of opportunity arose. Storm waves were cutting into the beach and washing out house planks, wooden halibut hooks, a harpoon shaft, parts of a carved box, and a canoe paddle. The Makah Tribal Council phoned Washington State University—and Richard Daugherty returned to Ozette and reopened the investigations. That was February 1970, and Daugherty anticipated working through the following summer. Instead, excavation has been under way continuously for eight years. From the beginning the Makah Indian Nation and the scientific team have worked together, Makah students taking part in the excavation and preservation of artifacts, Makah elders visiting the site and sharing memories. Everything recovered from the old houses will become part of a multi-million-dollar tribal museum newly built in Neah Bay.

Radiocarbon dating places the age of the buried houses at 450 B.P., well before the era of European exploration which began along the Washington coast in 1774 with the arrival of the Spaniard Juan Perez. The location of five houses of this age is known; excavation of three is nearly complete. An additional house dating to about 800 B.P. is apparent beneath the floor of one of these—a layer cake of time, with villagers building anew as mudflows and centuries took their toll.

Preservation is remarkable because the heavy wet clay of the slide sealed out air and prevented oxidation and decay. Animal tissue is gone except for bone—and a single braid of human hair in place on a hardwood bowl that is carved in the form of a man. Plant fiber and wood have remained intact. There even are wood chips marking a workshop area within one of the houses; and alder and twinberry leaves have been recovered still green, although they quickly darken and turn brown on exposure to the air.

Bone comb from the trench at Ozette (above). A photograph of the Ozette village (below) shows traditional shed-roofed houses. The picture must have been taken several years after the wreck of the ship Austria in 1877, judging from the condition of its hulk resting on the beach.

As artifacts are found they are categorized and entered into a computer that keeps track of variables including the precise location of each item. The printout listing the 42,000 objects recovered as of March 1978 fills a volume three inches thick. It includes entries such as: 1,056 baskets, 1,126 mats, 86 hats, 80 tumplines, 13 loom uprights, 114 halibut hook shanks, 954 arrow shafts, 110 harpoons, 78 tool handles, 14 chisels, 1,095 wedges, 776 box fragments, 99 bowls—and on and on, item by item, category by category. It is a look at the past never before possible, for no archaeological opportunity anywhere quite matches this one. The mudflow in effect stopped the clock at Ozette, leaving virtually everything preserved in place, somewhat as volcanic ash has preserved a record of everyday life in ancient Pompeii. At Ozette, however, the objects themselves remain, not just their molds. Recovering and preserving them has called for the development of new techniques.

Each of the houses was large—sixty to seventy feet long and about thirty-five feet wide. Several hearths indicated separate family cooking areas within each house, and split cedar sticks suggested fireside roasting like that of Makah barbecues today. Raised platforms ringed the walls, used for sleeping and for storage. Associated with them students found the greatest concentrations of artifacts, often jackstrawed into three-dimensional puzzles—for example, a bench with a sleeping mat still in place, a flattened box on top of the bench and crisscrossed beneath it a basket, a loom, a canoe paddle, two seal clubs, and a bow.

Evidently the ranking family of the first house to be excavated had lived in the left rear quarter, as figured from the single doorway facing the beach. Ceremonial gear and whaling harpoons were there. So was a cedar-bark hat woven with a decided knob at the crown, the traditional style of high-status persons.

Painstaking study of the physical remains of the buried houses allowed Ozette archaeologists to piece together considerable detail regarding the architecture of 500 years ago. Planks—as much as 1½ feet wide—were slung between upright posts, held in position with withes. This construction permitted disassembly of houses, a convenience in moving seasonally to take advantage of food resources at other locations. Note the roof boards overlapping in a manner similar to tiles to keep out rain, and the fish-drying racks at the back of the house.

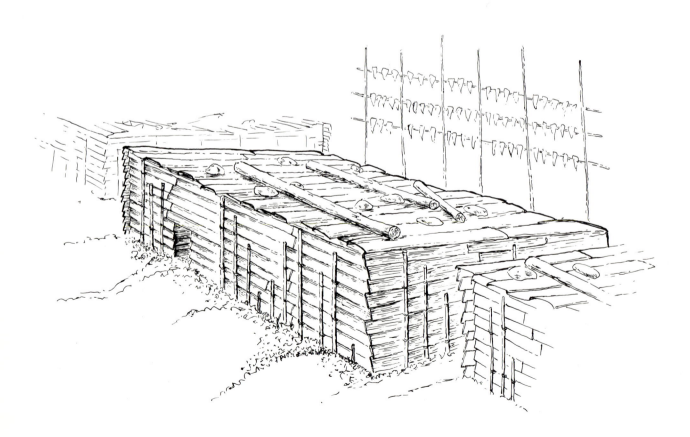

To excavate without damaging fragile items, Daugherty decided to use spray from hoses, gently washing away the mud of the centuries with water pumped from the ocean. Once removed from the ground, wood and fiber artifacts go quickly into a preservation bath of polyethylene glycol. It soaks into the waterlogged tissues and replaces the water with wax. In the case of objects already impregnated with oil such as hardwood bowls used for whale and seal oil—condiments for use with dried fish—this method hasn't worked well. Consequently, for these problem pieces, Gerald Grosso, conservator for the project, has adopted a technique of first removing the water with acetone, then impregnating the wood with rosin. To test an alternative method he flew one bowl to a laboratory in Australia for special freeze-drying. It was returned a few months later stabilized and ready for display, hand carried from Canberra by a conservator en route to Neah Bay for an international conference specially convened to discuss the preservation of waterlogged wood and fiber. So acclaimed is the Ozette undertaking that experts attended from the British Museum in London, from Sweden's famous project restoring the ship *Vasa*, from Ottawa's Museum of Man, the Smithsonian Institution, the Ivory Coast's Ministry of Science Research, the National Museum of Denmark, and so on.

Ozette offers not just architectural traces such as post molds and hearths, but entire houses; not just structures, but complete contents; and not just utilitarian and ceremonial objects, but items in all stages of manufacture and of repair. There are finished whalebone clubs and roughed-out blanks ready to be shaped and carved, delicately carved combs of wood and bone, also comb blanks with the teeth outlined but not yet cut through. There are bench planks that had accidently split in two and been repaired by drilling and lashing; a box patched with a piece of wood sewn in place to cover a hole; and the side of an old canoe and a whale scapula used as part of a house wall.

Identification of the materials of which artifacts are made demonstrates the knowledge of physical properties that the Ozette people had and the suitability of what they selected for the function it was intended to perform. For example, mussel-shell harpoon heads have been found broken off in both whale vertebrae and shoulder blades, testimony to the strength and sharpness of shell blades. Bowls are carved of red alder and Oregon ash, woods without strong resins that would be too flavorful; wedges are made from the dense compression wood of the underside of spruce branches, a readily obtainable material comparable in characteristics to the fairly rare yew wood reported ethnographically for wedges.

Halibut hooks and fur-seal bones in the deposits point to thousands of years of maritime technology. Whaling gear sings of humanity's urge to venture beyond the necessary. Decoration even of utilitarian objects—and petroglyphs pecked into beach boulders near the village—speak of the spirit world. Here were a people joined to a physical and ritual universe different from ours today and distinct in particulars even from that of Puget Sound villagers. Yet Ozette serves as a window to the past through which the commonality of mankind gleams with poignant clarity: economic needs, artistic impulses, metaphysical attunement—and also the fleeting nature of human life. For transcience is the legacy of all individuals and all cultures.

Archaeology's function is to make the past a part of the present. It lends perspective to the moment we hold as our own.

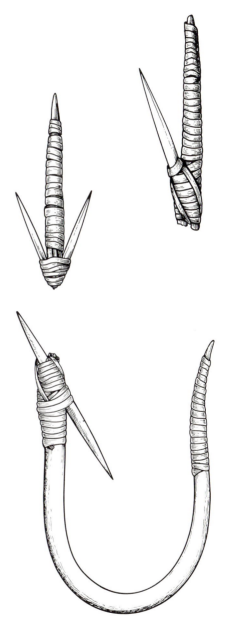

Hooks for codfish and halibut, Ozette. Wrappings are wild cherry bark; points are bone. Microscopic identification indicates western hemlock as the wood most commonly used for fishhooks.

Four petroglyph sites on the west coast of Vancouver Island and one at Sproat Lake show great similarity to the petroglyphs at Wedding Rock, two miles south of Ozette. No method of dating has yet been developed, but since several petroglyph motifs also are present on Ozette artifacts they may be contemporaneous with the buried houses. Although most of the Olympic coast petroglyphs are at Wedding Rock, some are on the beach close to the Ozette village site and a few are north of the Ozette River. Molds were made of forty-four petroglyphs, including several with composite motifs, as part of the Ozette–Makah museum program (below and opposite). Rock surfaces first were draped with protective plastic sheeting. Then quick-setting latex rubber was spread on, backed with burlap, left for a few hours, and peeled off. From these molds, casts of the petroglyphs were made for display in Neah Bay.

Round faces pecked into a boulder closely match decorative faces from the Ozette houses, including one on the handle of a metal-bladed chisel (top, left). A wolf design decorates the handle of a weaver's sword (above) and one of the petroglyphs, shown here as a finished mold (right). The depth of the incising and overall character of this particular petroglyph, however, may indicate it is more recent than the buried houses.

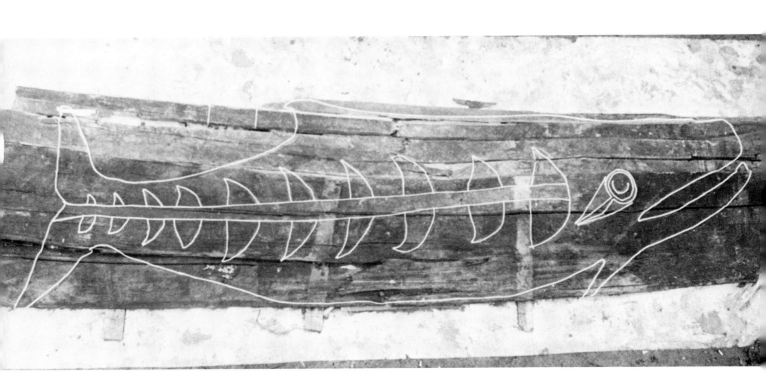

Whale motifs, present as petroglyphs (upper right) also were frequent within the Ozette houses. Two planks incised with whales evidently had served as decorative screens. The one shown here (above) was photographed with string laid into the carving to emphasize the lines.

Makah Indians today gather cedarbark in early
June when rising sap makes it peel easily. Outer
bark is stripped off and discarded. Inner bark is
dried in the sun, then stored in bundles. For use
in making baskets, pieces are thinned and split
to the desired width.

Baskets from the Ozette houses (left) indicate that historic basketry styles of the Olympic coast have changed little from those of several centuries ago. Contemporary Quileute Indians gather beargrass as weft material at Queets Prairie (below, left). It grows exceptionally long there, presumably in response to lowland conditions. Usually an alpine species, this beargrass is thought to be a glacial relict: it moved downslope as Pleistocene ice accumulated in the high Olympics, then remained in the lowlands as conditions moderated. Cattail also is used for baskets (below, right), and formerly mats were made of it as well.

Tools from the Ozette houses include chisels with blades of beaver teeth (top, right) and of steel (bottom). Presumably, the metal came across the Pacific Ocean from Japan on shipwrecked junks. A piece of bamboo about a foot long and four inches in diameter suggests trans-Pacific drift. Also present in the houses were adze handles similar to those in use by contemporary canoe makers (top).

Right and below: *Boxes bent from single pieces of kerfed wood which were pegged shut and fitted with bottoms and sometimes lids are characteristic of the Northwest coast. Replicating Ozette boxes, an archaeologist removed a prepared yellow cedar board from a bed of seaweed where it had been steaming with fire-heated rocks and water. He then folded it at each of three kerfs and tied it in position to cool. A box from House One is shown below at the left. Box uses ranged from containers to cooking (by adding hot rocks and water). Many were decorated by carving and inlaying animal teeth, or by painting.*

The bravery and skill that carried hunters to sea in canoes (above, photographed in the early 1900s) is demonstrated by the many indications of whaling present at Ozette. These include a large cedar carving of a whale fin, inlaid with more than 700 sea-otter teeth (below, left) and harpoon blades broken-off within whale vertebrae (below, right) and scapulae.

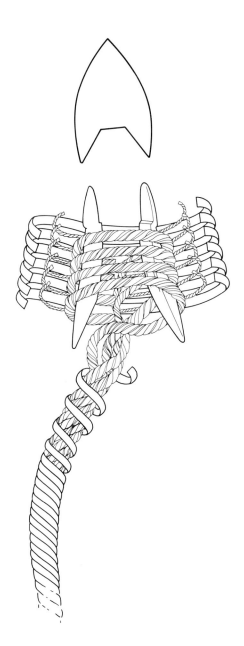

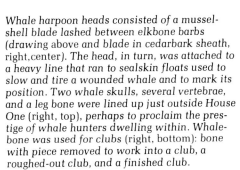

Whale harpoon heads consisted of a mussel-shell blade lashed between elkbone barbs (drawing above and blade in cedarbark sheath, right, center). The head, in turn, was attached to a heavy line that ran to sealskin floats used to slow and tire a wounded whale and to mark its position. Two whale skulls, several vertebrae, and a leg bone were lined up just outside House One (right, top), perhaps to proclaim the prestige of whale hunters dwelling within. Whale-bone was used for clubs (right, bottom): bone with piece removed to work into a club, a roughed-out club, and a finished club.

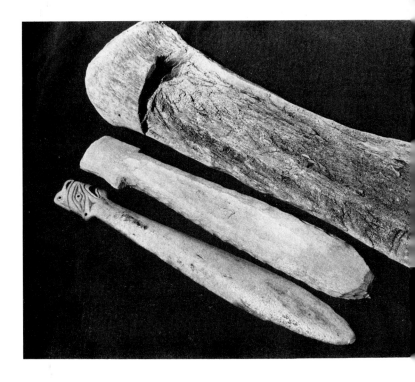

Opposite: *Ozette bowls used to hold seal and whale oil, favored as condiments, include one carved in human form complete to a braid of hair. A box front carved to represent the face of Thunderbird came from House Two. It seems to have been part of a box drum.*

Plaid blanket from Ozette woven of cedarbark and cattail fluff as an extender for dog wool (top, left). Wooden mat creaser used in making cattail mats (top, right). Wooden swords used in Ozette weaving (center). Replicated Ozette loom being tested by one of the Makah girls helping to excavate (left).

Ozette carvings in wood (above and opposite, top) and in bone (opposite, below). The eyes of the figure above continue around and become part of a similar face on the back.

Guide to Site Locations

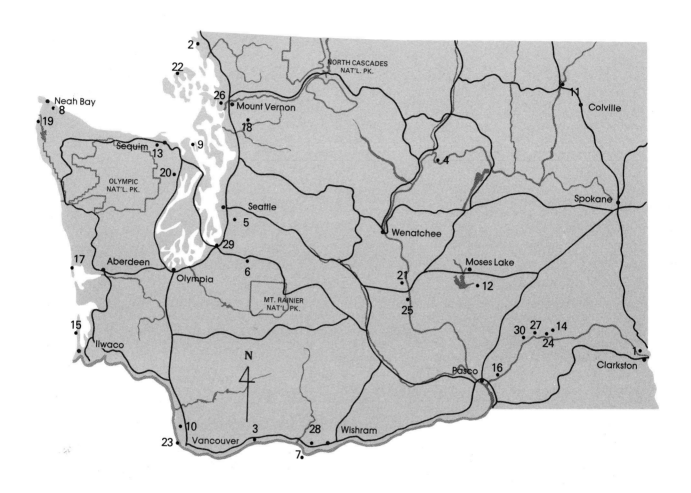

1. Alpowa	11. Kettle Falls	21. Ryegrass Coulee
2. Birch Bay	12. Lind Coulee	22. San Juan Island
3. Bonneville	13. Manis Mastodon	23. Sauvies Island
4. Chief Joseph	14. Marmes Rockshelter	24. Squirt Cave
5. Duwamish	15. Martin	25. Sunset Creek
6. Enumclaw Plateau	16. Miller	26. Swikwikwab
7. Five Mile Rapids	17. Minard	27. Three Springs Bar
8. Hoko River	18. Olcott	28. Wakemap
9. Indian Island	19. Ozette	29. Wapato Creek
10. Kersting	20. Quilcene	30. Windust Caves

Index

Marmes Man. *See* Marmes site
Marmes site: excavation at, 36-41; cremation hearth at, 40; rockfall, 56; soil peels, 13; mentioned, 92
Marrow, 38, 54, 73
Martin site, 88-89
Mastodon: and spearpoint, 26; compared with mammoth, 27-28, 30; range, 30; kill sites, 32. *See also* Extinction
Mehringer, Peter, palynologist, 28
Migration. *See* Salmon
Miller site, 71
Minard site, 88-89
Mobility: effects of, 70
Monoliths. *See* Columns
Mount Baker: ashfall from, 13
Mount Mazama: ashfall from, 13, 36, 56; mentioned, 9
Mount Rainier: ashfall from, 13. *See also* Osceola mudflow
Mount St. Helens: ashfall from, 13
Mudflow. *See* Kautz Creek mudflow; Osceola mudflow; Ozette site
Munsell, David, archaeologist, 67, 82, 83, 87
Mussel-shell harpoon blade, 95
Mussels. *See* Shellfish

Namu site, British Columbia, 84
Neah Bay, 93, 95
Needles: at Lind Coulee, 36; Marmes, 40
Net sinkers, 49, 84
Nets, 49, 86, 87, 88
Newberry Crater: ashfall from, 13

Obsidian: trade of, 11; sharpness of blades, 55
Ocean Shores site. *See* Minard site
Okanogan highlands: and ice, 14; pithouses, 69
Olcott sites, 82-83
Olivella shells, 37, 68
Onat, Astrida, archaeologist, 87
Osceola mudflow, 83
Oysters. *See* Shellfish
Ozette site: environmental character, 88, 90; compared with Martin and Minard sites, 89; abandoned, 92; houses, 92, 93, 94; mudflow, 94; conservation of artifacts, 95; mentioned, 88

Pasco: loess near, 11. *See also* Icebergs
Pestles; basalt, 81
Petersen, Kenneth, palynologist, 28
Petroglyphs, 95
Pipes: from Okanogan, 69
Pithouses, 69-72, 83
Plant foods, 67. *See also* Root digging
Pleistocene. *See* Glacier ice
Pleistocene fauna. *See* Extinction
Pollen: and archaeology, 28
Polyethylene glycol. *See* Preservation
Porpoises, 84
Port of Seattle. *See* Duwamish site
Port of Tacoma. *See* Wapato Creek site
Potlatch system, 89

Preservation: rock shelter, 10; wet-site, 28, 49, 83; in laboratory, 95
Prestige: and social system, 90. *See also* Social ranking
Prince Rupert region. *See* Namu site
Projectile points: design of, 66; at Alpowa, 72; willow leaf, 82; bone, 89. *See also* Atlatl; Bow and Arrow; Mastodon; Names of individual sites
Puget Lobe. *See* Glacier ice
Puget Sound: blocked by ice, 14-15

Queen Charlotte Islands, 84
Quilcene: Olcott site, 82-83

Radiocarbon dating, 13, 28, 83. *See also* Names of individual sites
Red tides, 85
Reef netting, 86
Rice, Harvey, archaeologist, 65-66
Rock shelters: cause of, 9; used by man, 10. *See also* Marmes site; Squirt Cave; Windust Caves
Roll, Tom, archaeologist, 89
Root digging, 73, 88
Rye grass: used with nets, 86

Salmon: migration of, 45; utilized by man, 46, 47, 94; in salt water, 86; vertebrae, 88
San Juan Island sites, 84
Sauvies Island: in Columbia River, 81
Schalk, Randall, archaeologist, 48, 71
Sea level: lowered, 15, 29, 82, 84
Sea lions: 84
Sea otters: 84
Sea urchins. *See* Shellfish
Seal: harbor, 88, 89; fur, 89, 95
Seasonal rounds, 73-74, 90
Sequim. *See* Icebergs; Manis mastodon site
Shellfish: human utilization of, 84, 85, 88
Shells: growth rings on, 85; indicate past environment, 87
Skagit River: delta expansion, 56; stone sculpture, 81. *See also* Swikwikwab site
Slaves. *See* Social ranking
Social ranking: Northwest Coast, 48, 89
Sockeye. *See* Salmon
Soil columns. *See* Columns
Soil peels. *See* Marmes site; Columns
Spears. *See* Mastodon; Weapons
Squirt Cave, 67
Status. *See* Prestige; Whaling
Stillaguamish River: and Olcott sites, 82
Stone: used by man, 52-53. *See also* Basalt; Obsidian
Stone tools: effectiveness of, 52, 54
Storage: of food, 48, 89, 90
Strait of Juan de Fuca: blocked by ice, 14; mentioned, 86. *See also* Hoko River site
Strawberry Island. *See* Miller site
Sturgeon: 90
Subsistence: relation to sites, 88. *See also* Seasonal rounds
Sunset Creek site, 69
Swikwikwab site, 87, 88
Suttles, Wayne, anthropologist, 89,90

Terraces, 82, 84
Three Springs Bar site, 69
Trade: evidence of, 37, 68; mentioned, 74
Traps: fish, 86

Vancouver, Washington: site near, 81
Volcanic ash, 9, 13, 56

Wakemap, 74, 81
Wapato Creek site, 87
Watercraft, 16, 84, 88, 90. *See also* Canoe travel
Waterfowl, 84, 88
Water screen, 40
Weapons: evolution of, 53. *See also* Attatl; Bow and Arrow
Weir, 48. *See also* Wapato Creek site
Whale: size of, 90
Whaling, 90
Willapa Bay. *See* Martin site
Windust Caves, 65

PHOTOGRAPHS by Ruth and Louis Kirk except as follows: Courtesy Helen Fryxell—10 (upper), 12, 14; Delbert Gilbow—11 (upper); Hoko River Project—48 (left), 49 (upper half of page), 60 (center), 61; Lind Coulee Project—22 (center left and right), 34, 35, project photo by Mike Short, 36; Rick McClure—62; Minard Project—57 (lower right), 88 (lower), 89; David Munsell—55 (lower), 86, 87; Courtesy Florence Nattinger—50 (lower); Oregon Archaeological Society—111 (clay face), 80 (lower), 81 (upper); Oregon Historical Society—111 (stone owl), 80 (upper), 81 (lower); Ozette Project—by Gerald Grosso, 91—by Mike Short, 112 (wooden faces), 75 (lower left), 102 (lower left), 106 (upper left and right), 107; Kenneth Petersen—19 (upper half of page); Harvey S. Rice—21 (lower left), 22 (upper), 39 (lower left), 44 (lower); 54 (left), 55 (right), 63 (lower), 99 (upper left); Mike Short— 78 (lower left); U.S. Army Corp of Engineers—66 (lower); Washington State Historical Society—93 (lower), 102 (upper); Yakima Public Library, Relander Coll.—76-77.

DRAWINGS by Chris Walsh, except pages 2-3 by Dale Croes.

GEOLOGY MAPS by A. Dan Horn with Yoshi Nishihara.

SITE LOCATION MAP by Yoshi Nishihara.

Bone, Ozette

Stone, Lower Columbia

Clay, Lower Columbia

Wood, Ozette